Fabric Traditions of Indonesia

Bronwen and Garrett Solyom

Washington State University Press
and
The Museum of Art, Washington State University
Pullman, Washington
1984

Published in conjunction
with the exhibition
Fabric Traditions of Indonesia
organized by the Museum of Art
Washington State University

Exhibited at
The Museum of Art
Washington State University
Pullman, Washington

November 6 through
December 16, 1984

and at
The Bellevue Art Museum
Bellevue, Washington

March 9 through
May 5, 1985

 Washington State University Press
Cooper Publications Building
Pullman, Washington 99164-5910

Printed and bound in the
United States of America
Washington State University Press
Pullman, Washington

Library of Congress
Cataloging in Publication Data

Solyom, Bronwen.
    Fabric traditions of Indonesia.

    Bibliography: p.
    1. Textile fabrics—Indonesia.
    I. Solyom, Garrett.
II. Title.
TS1413.I55S65 1984 677'.02864 84-22091
ISBN 0-87422-019-X

This publication and exhibition are made
possible in part with funds from: the National
Endowment for the Arts; the FRIENDS of the
Museum of Art at Washington State University; the Manring family; the United States
Agency for International Development Program Support Grant; and the Washington
Commission for the Humanities, a non-profit
organization supported by the National Endowment for the Humanities and by private
contributors.

*Cover illustrations (fig. 69): Stylized mythical
lizards and supplementary weft wrapping
decorate the ends of a ceremonial tube skirt
woven by a Tetum woman from the South
Belu area of Central Timor. Warp 124 cm,
weft 114 cm. Collection: Moss.*

*Fig. 52 (right): A horseback rider among the
betel vines is among the motifs found on an
18' holy cloth,* sarita, *from the Sa'dan Toraja
of Southwestern Sulawesi. Warp 555 cm, weft
22.5 cm. Private collection.*

CONTENTS

Fabric Traditions of Indonesia

FOREWORD

*"For the world is not to be narrowed till it will go into the
understanding . . . but the understanding is to be expanded and
opened till it can take in the image of the world."*

Francis Bacon (1561-1626)
The Parasceve

For the past five years Washington State University has forged ties with Indonesia through mutual involvement in a project to develop higher education in the Eastern Islands of the Republic. The project, funded by the United States Agency for International Development, is but one part of our university's international commitment. As a land-grant institution WSU has a mission to put its agricultural knowledge and other wide-ranging expertise to use for the benefit of the developing world.

In the case of Indonesia as with many other countries, such benefits have been by no means all in one direction. For not only have we welcomed scores of Indonesians and their families to our campus, but also our own faculty have come away from their time in Indonesia with experience of the richness of a culture previously unknown to them.

They, however, were the fortunate few. Those of us who remained behind had little opportunity to know about this fascinating nation of over 13,000 islands, arcing from Malaysia in the North to Australia in the West and sharing with our own state a place on the rim of the Pacific. For many of us the cultural diversity of Indonesia, its economic as well as artistic strength, its several religions, numerous languages and large and varied population, the fifth largest in the world, were all well-kept secrets.

When the Museum of Art at Washington State University first considered an exhibition of the arts and cultures of Indonesia, we were particularly conscious of the role we could play in bringing to our campus and community some of the richness and diversity of that distant nation. Such a purpose was seen as central to our aims. As part of an educational institution, and a singularly visible part at that, we too are working to encourage the growth of an international perspective. Our approach is not based on the more usual international curricular areas of commerce, technology, science, and politics, but on the arts and humanities. For it is through these that the understanding of other cultures is often best begun. And to understand another's culture, to respect its integrity, is to have taken a major stride. In the words of WSU Provost Albert C. Yates: "We can never hope to allay our fears of future global conflict . . . or live tranquilly as good neighbors, without greater emphasis on informing ourselves about cultures different from our own."*

The potential of museums should not be overlooked in this quest. No longer merely the static repositories of the past, museums have begun to assume an active role as communicators of cultural heritage—often in a manner that can illuminate and even affect the present. Whether it be in this country or abroad, at the local or national level, museums fill a need to nourish an understanding of the world—both the world beyond their doors and that beyond their shores. It is no coincidence that the last triennial meeting of the International Committee on Museums in 1983 chose as its theme "Museums for the Developing World."

Such goals are nothing, however, without the tangible means to realize them. Museums deal, after all, with abstract ideas expressed through the concrete example. At the WSU Museum of Art our particular good fortune was to discover within close reach one such example—an outstanding collection of textiles from Indonesia in the possession of an alumnus of our university, Timothy Manring, and his wife, Indrastuti Hadiputranto. The collection, made during several years of living in Indonesia, became the nucleus of our exhibition and the seed from which a whole program of other interpretative events has sprung, encouraged by the openness and sharing attitude of the Manrings. Subsequently we have

Fig. 54 (left): A version of the Central Javanese batik semen *pattern. Here traditional motifs such as mountains and pavilions have been combined to become an elaborate hourglass shape reminiscent of the Balinese* cili *figure, associated with the rice goddess Dewi Sri. Warp 262 cm, weft 105.5 cm. Private collection.*

built on their collection with pieces borrowed from several equally generous individuals and public institutions in Washington State. In the process we have discovered on our very doorstep an unanticipated wealth of Indonesian textiles, most of them never previously exhibited, plus a concomitant interest in and knowledge of the subject. At the suggestion of our authors, Bronwen and Garrett Solyom, these local collections have been supplemented by a few pieces from further afield, to provide vital links in some of the conclusions reached in this publication.

But why textiles? Because traditional textiles are widely recognized as among the greatest artistic achievements of Indonesia. They are the chief form of artistic expression throughout almost all of the Archipelago, diverse though those forms of expression might be. They have an immense beauty, great decorative value, and a high degree of sophisticated skill in the various techniques of dyeing and weaving. Their aesthetic qualities, use of color, pattern and motif make them of special appeal to a modernist, Western eye, which has learned to appreciate as art many materials once only to be found in ethnographic study collections.

However, the textiles of Indonesia are also an important key to the culture of that country. They have a central role in many of the rituals associated with life's passages—birth, initiation, marriage, and death. Their content, technique, and materials reflect a diversity of histories, religions, and political systems as well as social and practical needs. Their purposes range from the mundane to the cosmic, but above all they are artistic creations in the true Asian sense of art—they are made to be used. It is precisely because of their centrality to life that the arts of Indonesia can provide a means for understanding the culture of that country.

We intend that our presentation should be aesthetically pleasing in its own right but also serve the purpose of an introduction to many aspects of the culture of Indonesia. An additional purpose is to add in a modest way to the scholarship on Indonesian textiles. Garrett and Bronwen Solyom, who have not only written the text of this work but have also played a major role in the selection process, are using an approach with a new focus. They have organized their observations thematically and not in the normal geographic fashion, island-by-island, west-to-east, so that the connections between imagery, technique, and materials may more clearly be seen. They have looked at the evolution of textiles in Indonesia linked to non-loom traditions such as painted bark-cloth, beadwork, and plaitwork. Through their text we hope that new insights may be gained into the nature of these textiles and their role in the culture.

This publication is but one part, albeit the only permanent one, of a much larger whole. Conceived around the catalogue and exhibition is an interdisciplinary and interpretative program of performances, technical demonstrations, lectures and films. Through this diversified yet coordinated approach we hope to provide the possibility of a fuller understanding of the richness of Indonesia's arts and cultures. To this end the exhibit has been augmented by maps and explanatory photographs as well as implements and carvings not only associated with the making and use of textiles but with other areas of Indonesian life and arts. Scholars from this university and elsewhere have lent to the project their expertise, whether it be in the areas of anthropology, art history, Asian studies, textile history, international studies, music or theatre. Personnel from our university's A.I.D. project in Indonesia have contributed advice and insights and enough excellent photographs for us to make the introductory videotape "Unity in Diversity: The Arts and Cultures of Indonesia." *Wayang* and gamelan performers have brought to life mythical personnages and placed them squarely in the 20th century. Films such as Fons Rademaker's *Max Havelaar* have led to discussions of politics and colonial rule, while other documentary films have examined questions of religion and social customs. Above all, our Indonesian friends, especially the members of *Permias* (the Indonesian Student Association in the United States), have assisted with advice and enthusiasm, and often intrigued by the diversity of their own cultural heritage, have responded with continual goodwill to this attempt by foreigners to portray their native land.

If we have succeeded in building up a picture of Indonesian culture through these various programs and have revealed the visual splendor of Indonesia's traditional textiles, it is at best a start. All our efforts can only provide a pale reflection of the reality of Indonesia's cultural wealth and diversity.

This project reflects the invaluable support of many individuals and organizations who have contributed to its success. Bronwen and Garrett Solyom in Honolulu have been unstinting in their enthusiasm, time, and scholarship as authors and curators. Private collectors in this state and elsewhere have generously loaned pieces for our exhibition, as have also several public institutions. In Washington, D.C. we owe a special debt of gratitude to the Embassy of the Republic of Indonesia, in particular to His Excellency A. Hasnan Habib and Dr. Sambas Wirakusumah, as well as to Mattiebelle Gittinger, Research Associate in Indonesian Textiles for the Textile Museum. (Indeed, to Dr. Gittinger the scholarship on Indonesian textiles in general owes a very special debt.) In Santa Cruz, at the University of California, we have benefited from the expertise of Kathy Foley, dalang, as well as Undang Sumarna, Henry Spiller, Carol Panofsky, and Herman and Suzanne Suwanda from the university's gamelan. Closer to home in Seattle, Dan and Arlene Lev, Diana Ryesky, Krista Jensen Turnbull, Judy Sourakli, and above all, Mrs. Paul Ewbank, have gone out of their way to make our task a pleasure. At Washington State University in Pullman, we extend thanks to a myriad of colleagues: Osman Lewangka and Moira and Jahja Hanafie from *Permias;* Mary Finney and Jim Henson from the Office of International Program Development; Jean Klopfer from the Department of Clothing, Interior Design and Textiles; Burl Yarberry, Martin Waananen and many others from WSU's Eastern Islands Agricultural Education Project; Fred Bohm and Jo Savage from our University Press; as well as Mignon Perry, Alice Spitzer, Mark Fleisher, Fritz Blackwell, and Bob Harder. Other invaluable assistance in Pullman has come from: Kathleen Ferrington and the Neill Public Library; Nancy Johansen and the Palouse Weavers' Guild; Betty H. and Allen Manring; Phyllis Vettrus; Mary Alice Dickinson; the Palouse Chapter of the Society for International Development; and our ever-supportive FRIENDS of the Museum of Art. At the Museum itself special thanks are due to my former colleague, Barbara Coddington, without whom this venture might not have survived, and to Sanford Sivitz Shaman, Margaret Johnson, Joyce Irwin, Marc Fleisher, Pamela Awana Lee, Suzanne LeBlanc, Scott Stewart, and Mike Sletten.

Patricia Grieve Watkinson, Curator and Acting Director

A Special Challenge to the Modern University, WSU-IPDO, occasional paper 2, 1984.

Fabric Traditions of Indonesia

The Traditions and Their Beginnings

Indonesian fabrics are so surprisingly diverse in technique, materials, and appearance that they expand our usual notions of the meaning of the word "fabric." The hundreds of ethnic groups that inhabit the resource-filled tropical islands of the Indonesian Archipelago have produced a multitude of loom-woven textiles from everyday cottons to rich ceremonial silks. But they have also created many non-loom products. These include: bark-cloth; plaitwork mats, head covers, and containers; effigy figures created from various fibers; even architectural elements such as thatching and panels for house walls. All can be described as fabrics, literally "fibrous constructions."[1] Beyond the plainer mats and more utilitarian baskets there is a sophistication and artistry equal to that found in loom-woven textiles. Recent exhibitions and publications have emphasized Indonesian loom-woven textiles, but in their cultural context these textiles form only part of a greater world of Indonesian fabrics.

The peoples of each Indonesian region have their own distinctive traditional dress, often plain for daily use and more elaborate for ceremonial and ritual occasions. Religious and agricultural festivals or such rites of passage as initiations, circumcisions, tooth filings, weddings, and funerals provide the most impressive view of fabrics in use as both ritual accoutrements and costume. They are frequently worn with elaborate jewelry and headdresses, which often utilize the same motifs as the fabrics and have the same symbolic significance.

As long as the Indonesian islands have been peopled there have been fabrics, but what fabrics came first, what followed, and when, can only be surmised, as the evidence is tantalizingly incomplete. In prehistoric Southeast Asia, before loom-weaving was developed, various population groups exploited a wealth of local fiber materials and developed bark-cloth, cordage, and plaitwork that met their needs and satisfied their ritual and expressive sensibilities. Very likely, the art of tattooing complemented these fabric traditions: patterns used as tattoo motifs have been employed on plaitwork and sculpture, and sometimes on woven textiles.

In the course of prehistoric migrations this basic knowledge of fabrics and tattooing was probably carried from Southeast Asia and spread through the Pacific. Some broad sense of the fabric traditions that existed in prehistoric Southeast Asia can be gained from considering the fabrics that continue to be made in Oceania, especially in those areas that had no looms or metal until the arrival of Europeans in the eighteenth century. People in these areas achieved and preserved a high degree of technical and artistic sophistication in their cordage, bark-cloth, and plaitwork, unlimited and unaffected by a technical and cultural bias toward the loom and its flat, finished products.

There are still strong traditions associated with cordage in the Pacific. As a material for fastening and binding almost anything from canoes to houses, cordage had practical significance that gave it economic and cultural importance. Compacted lengths, large balls, or even carefully measured bundles of fine cordage were used as currency, or as a medium of ritual exchange. Important religious images were also made of cordage.[2] In Southeast Asia, the early availability of metal and the widespread use of bamboo may have stunted the development of a parallel cordage tradition, although early cord-marked pottery from Borneo[3] and images from the Batak people of north Sumatra that contain a large component of cordage[4] are known to exist.

Sophisticated bark-cloth and plaitwork exist in mainland and island Southeast Asia today, but less prominently. At some prehistoric time such technologies were eclipsed by the development of loom-woven textiles and the arrival of imported cloth. These events expanded the range of possibilities that now form the greater and better known part of Indonesia's fabric traditions.

The earliest evidence for weaving in Southeast Asia comes from Yunnan Province in southwestern China, from the sites of Shizhaishan and Lizhaishan, dated to the Western Han Empire (206 B.C.-A.D. 8) and identified with a non-Chinese culture more closely related culturally to Southeast Asia. At both sites, bronze loom parts for foot-braced, body-tension (back-strap) looms have been identified. In addition, at Shizhaishan, a sculpture on the lid of a bronze cowrie container shows six women weaving on foot-braced looms.[5] The full-sized loom parts and other sewing and weaving implements found are both refined and sophisticated, suggesting that the technology for their use was already well established by that time.

Unfortunately, there is no archaeological evidence available to date or chart the spread of this technology. Foot-braced, body-tension looms exist in scattered nineteenth and twentieth century locations on three sides of Indonesia, including Taiwan, Assam, South Viet-

Spelling: Indonesian orthography has undergone several significant revisions. The latest spelling is used in this publication.

Technical terms: See Glossary.

Measurements: Unless otherwise specified, the longest measurement along each dimension is given, including fringes, etc.

Dating: It is difficult to date Indonesian textiles on stylistic or technical grounds alone, or on physical condition. In the tropics a textile made five years ago and regularly used can become very worn and "antique," while treasured heirloom pieces can be preserved so carefully that they appear relatively new. Sometimes part of an old textile, e.g. beadwork, will be recycled on a new foundation. Some textiles are obviously "old," being part of a weaving or dyeing tradition that has died out. Disconcertingly, manufacture of some of these textiles is being revived for commercial purposes. Furthermore, relatively early commercial copies of traditional Indonesian textiles, particularly batiks, were traded throughout the Indies by the Dutch and absorbed into local traditions. These are old textiles, yet not indigenous. Unless specific dating information is provided, textiles are assigned to: late 19th or early 20th century; pre-World War II; and post-World War II. Textiles for which no dating information is provided are assumed to fall into this last category.

Borneo: Present-day Borneo belongs politically to Indonesia, Malaysia, and Brunei. Because tribal groups currently extend, or once migrated, across political borders, textiles from both Indonesian Borneo (Kalimantan) and Malaysian Borneo (Sarawak and Sabah) are included here.

Fig. 2: A Sumbanese woman draws yarn from a hank of cotton, using the age-old drop spindle, here made of heavy, dense wood. Her arms and hands are tattooed with roosters, lions, etc.—motifs also found on Sumbanese textiles. Indigo mixed with lime is both the dye for the textiles and the ink for the tattoos. Field photograph, Prai Liu village, nr. Waingapu, Menno van Wyk, 1977.

Fig. 3: Stylized crocodiles are among the few motifs found on warp ikat skirts and jackets from the Lower Mahakam River region of East Kalimantan. Known also as "Kutei" ikats, they are made primarily of twisted and knotted leaf fibers. The motifs have an angular and semi-abstracted quality that distinguishes them from other Borneo substyles. The bodies are filled with small rectangles reminiscent of basket- or plaitwork. Warp 96.5 cm, weft 54 cm. Collection: Grace.

Fig. 1: Seated at her loom a weaver pauses in her work to suckle her child. Representing perhaps an ancestral mother and weaver, this important cast bronze sculpture raises questions about loom development in Indonesia. The foot-braced, body-tension loom depicted here is not known in the Indonesian Archipelago, except for Sarmi. The very existence of this sculpture suggests the cultural importance attributed to the weaver. Height: about 28 cm. Field photograph, Flores, Marie Jeanne Adams, 1968.

nam, Hainan, and the Bismarck Archipelago.[6] Yet apart from Sarmi in Irian Jaya, none are known from Indonesia. This absence makes a mysterious cast bronze sculpture found in Flores all the more enigmatic (fig. 1). A mother, at work at her foot-braced, body-tension loom, takes a moment to suckle her child. The figure apparently had not been buried but was kept as a family heirloom.[7] Although its origin and age are unknown, this sculpture may represent an aspect of early weaving in eastern Indonesia.

There is no evidence that the foot-braced, body-tension loom is any earlier than other types of body-tension looms found in Indonesia. The first visual representation of a loom in Indonesia appears in a relief from Trowulan, the site associated with the capital of the fourteenth century East Javanese kingdom of Majapahit, and shows a girl weaving in an open pavilion.[8] The loom is clearly back-strap (not foot-braced), with a lozenge-patterned textile on it.

The varied tropical environments of the islands provided many sources of plant fibers that could have been used for weaving, although which were used first has not yet been determined. The earliest evidence so far, from mainland Southeast Asia, is ambiguous. The reports of the Shizhaishan findings unfortunately did not specify the kind of fibers remaining on bobbins that were found in sewing boxes at the site. Other finds included a bronze object that has been identified as a "hemp retting comb" and spindle whorls, the weights used at the end of drop spindles.[9] It is not clear whether the whorls would have been used for spinning bast fiber bundles or cotton. The same question applies to an object interpreted as a spindle whorl, found in a Ban Chiang site in northeast Thailand with an earlier date, 1000-300 B.C.[10] This might have been used for spinning yarn for weaving or cord for netting. There is so far no similar archaeological evidence for Indonesia. The introduction of Old World Indian cotton (*Gossypium arboreum*) into Indonesia is postulated to have occurred between two and three thousand years ago; however, wild New World cotton (*Gossypium hirsutum*) may also have been present as early as three thousand years ago.[11] With cotton available so early, the development of spinning and the use of both Old and New World cotton fibers could have occurred concurrently with the use of other fibers, although not necessarily in the same places. The drop spindle is still in use today (fig. 2) although the spinning wheel has long been available. Twisted or knotted bast as well as leaf and seed fibers have been widely used in Indonesia, from sources such as banana, pineapple, several palms, nettle, sago, and milkweed. They are often thought of as representing more archaic textile forms (fig. 3). Some are found, however, in conjunction with weaving techniques that require more than a minimal back-strap loom, such as supplementary weft pieces from Sangihe made of *kofo* from the leaf-sheath of a banana (*Musa textilis*).

Bark-cloth

Archaeologists theorize that bark-cloth was part of a cluster of so-called neolithic traditions that spread to Indonesia some time before 1000 B.C.[12] Although reliable archaeological evidence has yet to be recorded for Indonesia, a bark-cloth beater dated to about 700 B.C. has been found in the Philippines.[13]

One of the earliest records pertaining to bark-cloth in Indonesia is the Sarwadharma, a charter inscribed on seven bronze plates dated to A.D. 1269. It grants the clergy of a Shivaite religious domain (*dharma*) the right to cultivate paper mulberry trees (*Broussonetia papyrifera*). This was probably for the manufacture of a fine bark-cloth for clothing.[14] In Old Javanese such bark-cloth was called *daluwang,* a term that could also mean bark-cloth clothing, or head cloth. In thirteenth and fourteenth century East Java, while ordinary bark-cloth might have continued in use outside the courts,[15] the fine *daluwang* clothing apparently "belonged in the sacral sphere. The material was no longer generally worn in everyday life, but its use subsisted in the circles of religiously minded people, for making a kind of sacerdotal frocks."[16] There is no direct evidence that bark-cloth clothing was patterned, but *daluwang* was so fine that its surface might have been used for drawing and painting, and it was probably the "paper" on which the *wayang beber* were painted.[17]

With the Islamization of Java, many East Javanese customs were carried to neighboring Bali, which remained a Hindu enclave in a changing Southeast Asian world. Old Javanese painting traditions may well be perpetuated in the Balinese custom of painting astrological calendars and illustrating myths and legends to adorn courts and temples. The earliest extant examples are on bark-cloth (fig. 4) rather than cotton. It is not known if bark-cloth was made in Bali. In the nineteenth century it was imported mainly from Sulawesi,[18] perhaps

*Fig. 4: In this Hindu-Balinese bark-cloth painting (*gambaran*), disembodied heads are arranged around a central motif, possibly the sun. The heads may represent lightning. The birds are perhaps the phoenix or peacock. The piece was probably suspended by its corners from the ceiling of a shrine during temple festivals. Such painting on bark-cloth is the last remnant of an Old Javanese tradition. 127 x 125.8 cm. Collection: Museum of Cultural History, UCLA.*

Fig. 5: Made of two layers of fine bark-cloth and stained or dyed dark brown, this woman's blouse (lemba) has bast fiber stitchery at the wrist, neck, and waist and is patterned with glittering, crushed mica glue-work. It would have been worn with a voluminous bark-cloth or cotton skirt by the Toraja women of Central Sulawesi. Late 19th or early 20th century; 70 x 96 cm. Collection: Kahlenberg.

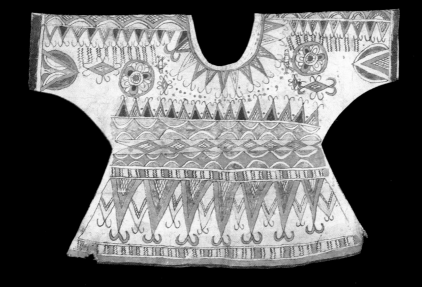

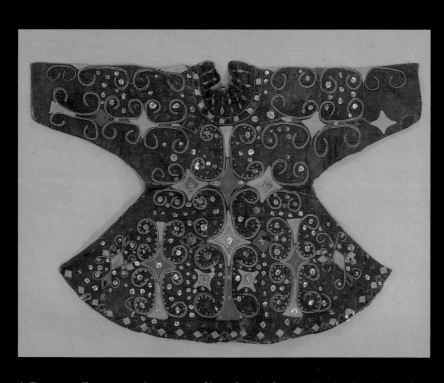

Fig. 6 (above): Paper mulberry was the source of bast for the finest white bark-cloth made by the Toraja. It provided a smooth surface for painting or stamping. The brilliant colors were once derived from vegetable sources. In this woman's blouse, among the traditional "flying bird," floral, and geometric motifs are the pan-Southeast Asian triangular repeats known as tumpal, *and unusual human figures. Pre-WWII; 45 x 67 cm. Collection: Moss.*

Fig. 8 (below): This Toraja woman's blouse is indigo-dyed cotton, appliquéd with pieces of red and yellow cloth and bright mica flakes secured with colorful embroidery. It shares the bold dramatic effect of its bark-cloth counterparts and a suggestion of the same motifs. It is lined with fine, brown bark-cloth, perhaps evidence of a slow transition from the use of bark-cloth to the complete adoption of cotton. Pre-WWII; 61 x 72.5 cm. Collection: Kahlenberg.

Fig. 7: *In some Indonesian societies, headhunting was once a ritual essential to the maintenance of community well-being. Within traditional cosmological belief systems, it was thought to ensure the proper advancement of life-death-life cycles, as well as agricultural and tribal fertility. The successful headhunter was recognized by the award of rising social rank, special accoutrements, tattoos, garments, and motifs. The Toraja head cloth (*siga*) of beaten bark, when worn at headhunting feasts by successful headhunters, may have had such cosmological associations.*

This example is divided into concentric squares, a representation of the universe. The center motif is based on stylized horned buffalo heads in a radiating arrangement that perhaps symbolizes the sun. The surrounding motifs, schematic four-pointed stars and four-petaled flowers, also reflect aspects of the upper and lower worlds of the Toraja people. Pre-WWII; 75 x 73 cm. Collection: Moss.

Fig. 9: The visual attraction of the shining surface of this small textile, from the Lampung region of South Sumatra, suggests its ceremonial role, perhaps as a cover to be displayed over food items used in ritual gift exchanges between families.

It appears to combine several archaic design traditions. The four-way symmetry with concentric four-petaled lotuses(?) and the octagonal band filled with birds and flowers suggest Buddhist, possibly even Persian, influence. The silk embroidery, couched silver metallic yarns, and appliquéd mica or mirror pieces are similar to the embroidered panels of some tube skirts, tapis, from the Lampung region, while the bright red commercial cloth border is probably an imported embellishment.

The textile is backed with thick red-brown bark-cloth which, besides being a sturdy support, may carry ritual or symbolic associations of its own, harking back to days when bark-cloth was more widely used. Late 19th or early 20th century; 64.5 x 63.5 cm. Collection: Leland.

because supplies of *daluwang* could no longer be obtained easily from Java. Bark-cloth was apparently not used in this pictorial story-telling function elsewhere in Indonesia or in the Pacific islands.

In more recent historical times, the use of bark-cloth has been recorded from many peoples on other islands.[19] But today, it has been displaced by cotton goods almost everywhere. Yet the Mentawai Island men still prefer their bark-cloth loin cloths,[20] and the cloth is still made by the Murut in Borneo and apparently some Toraja peoples in Central Sulawesi.[21]

Bark-cloth for daily use was plain or decorated very simply. It was also valued for special ritual functions, as in the following situation from Borneo. Hans Schärer quotes A. W. Nieuwenhuis:

> Among the Kenyah, the operation [tattooing] . . . must take place in a hut built specifically for the purpose. During the whole period of tattooing, male members of the family must dress in bark-cloth . . . .

Schärer comments:

> Tattooing is an initiation rite, and like other such rites it consists of a passing away and a new becoming, a death and a life. This is why the men put aside their usual clothes and assume bark-cloth, like widowed persons who wear clothes of the same material after the death of a husband or wife until the mortuary feast has been held and they too have been saved from death and have come back to life. After the tattooing is all over, the bark-cloth is put aside and new clothes are put on.[22]

Because they have been among the last to go, the bark-cloth traditions of the Toraja of Central Sulawesi are some of the best documented. The East Toraja (Bare'e), for example, traditionally did not weave, but believed they were predestined to make bark-cloth:

> When . . . the peoples of the Celebes separated . . . and each people obtained an implement that would determine its industry, the East Toradja received a stone hammer with which to beat tree bark. It is told that the art was learned from Roemongi, the wife of the legendary hero Lasaeo; according to others, it is supposed to have been her daughter, Ana-ntali, who, as the first woman, practiced this art.[23]

However, among Christianized Bare'e, the prescribed use of bark-cloth at sacrificial feasts and other occasions honoring the old gods fell into disuse. Certain beliefs lingered on, however: that the female leader of the harvest be dressed in bark-cloth, that a corpse be wrapped in at least one piece, and that a widow wear a bark-cloth headband, jacket, or shawl as a sign of her widowhood.[24]

From the various Toraja districts where bark-cloth was made, a range of techniques is demonstrated. On women's blouses are found needlework and mica glue-work (fig. 5); braided strips of bark-cloth for cuffs and collars; applied beads, cotton cloth, and contrasting colors of bark-cloth in geometric arrangements. More often the blouses are dyed, or painted freehand in brilliant colors (once from natural sources, later chemical) mainly red-pink, yellow, purple, and black (fig. 6). The geometric and stylized curvilinear motifs are seen in other painted bark-cloth items: sarongs, ponchos, shawls, betel bags, and women's stiffened headbands. The same strong colors are found on men's head cloths (fig. 7) that bear motifs related to headhunting achievements.[25] Apparently this painting was done by priestesses, or a certain class of men who dressed and lived like women.[26]

Bark-cloth also served a utilitarian function as sturdy backing or lining material for fabrics of other kinds. When the Toraja began to use bright cottons for their blouses, they retained the motifs and sometimes kept a bark-cloth liner to secure the layers of applied cloth and embroidery (fig. 8). Coarse red-brown bark-cloth was sometimes used in Sumatra as a backing for ceremonial cloths (fig. 9). Given the miscellaneous religious and ritual affiliations of bark-cloth briefly mentioned above, it is possible that its presence as a liner had sacred, as well as practical, purposes.

Mats and Plaitwork Traditions

Fig. 10: From a quantity of piled, swirling strips of red, black, and natural split rotan, *a mat takes shape under the nimble fingers of an Iban woman. She has begun the diagonal, single-layer structure from one corner, and a schematic pattern is emerging. Food would be laid out on these mats for guests at ceremonial feasts. Field photograph, Sarawak, Wilhelm G. Solheim II, 1963.*

" . . . Layers or strips of vegetable material arranged, sometimes carefully interwoven, as a cover or wrapper, occurring under or around skeletons or even coffins, part or whole." This is a description of the earliest matting known from the Indonesian Archipelago. It was found in an extended burial at the Niah Cave site in Sarawak and carbon-dated to approximately 1400 B.C. The matting was not scientifically analyzed but was thought to be either a kind of riverine bullrush or pandanus.[27] Much later, the use of mats in Java is recorded in the Chinese dynastic history for the T'ang dynasty (A.D. 618-906): " . . . even the largest houses are covered with palmleaves. They have couches of ivory, and mats of the outer skin of bamboo."[28] Apparently, mats were highly valued, enough to be included in the exotic tribute sent to China from Java. The annals of the Sung dynasty (A.D. 960-1279) record one shipment of gifts that included "rattan mats plaited with figures."[29] The use of mats in Java is confirmed by the Chinese traveler Ma Huan, who visited the kingdom of Majapahit in 1433 and noted that the people spread matting made of fine *rotan* or of patterned grass on the floors of their houses and sat cross-legged on them.[30] From these scattered observations comes evidence of a long history of mats being made of a variety of materials, for several functions, some figured or patterned, and accorded a degree of importance.

Sometimes mats rather than textiles became the primary vehicles of expression for the most deeply held religious beliefs or world views. Such mats have significance far beyond the everyday, practical level. The peoples of Borneo, including the Punan and Iban, are fine mat makers (fig. 10). The large complex mats made by the Ot Danum and Ngaju Dayak groups of Central and South Kalimantan are examples of some of the most powerful of all such sacred mats. They represent aspects of the complex Dayak world view which in general terms includes an upper world with its male deity (symbolized by the hornbill) and a lower world with its female deity (represented by the water snake).[31] A small vocabulary of motifs arranged in various combinations are found on the major mats. Some include a pictorial scene (fig. 11).[32] Seven of these sacred mats with the water snake motif, when laid one on top of another at the Ngaju wedding ceremony, represent the underworld from which new life comes. They are placed in a "room made with cloth in the center of the house and supplied with a 'cloth sky'." A gong filled with rice, topped with a coconut, a spear, and a small shrub hung with ornaments, is set on the mats. Together these objects ritually represent the "totality of the divine world" before which the ceremony takes place.[33]

The importance attributed to certain mats in Sumatra is illustrated by the fine eyelet or open-work mats of the Batak of Asahan. The end and side borders of these pandanus sleeping mats are decorated with geometric patterns of small holes, creating a delicate lace-like effect. According to tradition, this fine art was learned from a legendary princess and culture heroine, Nan Jomba Ilak. She was:

> . . . born a lizard, to the great distress of her parents. At her request a home was made for her in a great banyan tree in the forest of spirits where the great spirit Radja Tumording held sway. Here she lived with a cloud spirit as her companion, sometimes assuming the form of a beautiful princess, but resuming the form of a lizard when alarmed. She received as visitors the seven daughters of the spirit king, Radja Tumording, and taught them the art of weaving beautiful mats . . . she also made presents of her handiwork for her own parents, sending them by the cloud spirit as messenger.[34]

Thus, the art of making eyelet mats came to the Asahan Batak women and, when one died, her mat would be hung over her grave.[35]

From South Sumatra comes a ceremonial mat in which the motifs have been burned into the surface (fig. 12). The mat is not plaited, but made of strips of split *rotan*, laid parallel and skewered tightly together by strips that are threaded through at right angles, at intervals of about two inches. This construction technique is also used in Sarawak by the Kayan, Kenyah, and Kelabit.[36] In both places the mats are called *lampit*, also a Javanese word. *Lampit* were once used in the Sundanese court of Bantam, West Java. They are of various sizes, roll conveniently, and last a long time. Usually they are unpatterned, or at most, striped by the addition of a few strips of black *rotan*. In South Sumatra, even plain *lampit* were given ceremonial status. Apparently they were made by men, and when paired with *tampan*, a ceremonial cloth woven by women, the two expressed a male and female duality that was appropriately present in numerous ritual contexts. *Lampit* were sometimes used, for example, as sitting mats by brides during part of the wedding ceremony, by boys during circumcision, or by important elders attending significant meetings. At funerary rites they were sometimes

Fig. 11: *Among the Ot Danum of south central Kalimantan, ceremonial* rotan *mats such as this would appear at special feasts. Sacred gongs and prestige possessions such as* martaban, *giant ceramic storage jars, would be displayed upon them. Only heroes and other famous people would be permitted to sit on them.*

The motifs probably depict scenes from the upper world and the obstacle-laden journey of the soul of a deceased person attempting to reach it. Some of the trees are hung with gongs and other offerings given at the funeral feast to ensure the soul's entry to heaven. However, if a person had behaved badly in life, the soul might not get through the mountains with wild animals and "quivering" trees set to entrap it or pass by the guardian spirit that reviews its misdeeds.

The snake-like forms in the center are éhing. *In one myth of the region, they have been interpreted as rulers of the fish of heaven and are attracted to a heavenly fish trap, probably represented on the mat by the triangle filled with gongs (circles) at their heads. This is constructed by souls who have reached heaven, who will be enriched by the wealth of their agate fish scales. Because* éhing *are regarded also as having magic powers, offerings are made to them in times of danger or sickness. Alternatively, these* éhing *may be seen as representing the mythic water snakes that dwell in the primeval waters of the underworld and represent the female aspect of the cosmos. They are sometimes found in paintings by the neighboring Ngaju Dayak where they represent the very fountain of the earth. 190 x 117 cm. Collection: Museum of Cultural History, UCLA.*

Fig. 12: *The design on this* rotan *mat (*lampit*) from the Lampung region of South Sumatra is burned into the surface— a decorative technique little used in Indonesia but well suited to the hard, shiny* rotan. *The orientation of the motifs in the quadrants is such that the mat has no obvious right way up—appropriate for a sitting mat rather than a wall display. The pairing of erect and inverted ships to form an octagon is a design detail also found on* tampan. *The arrangement of the remaining motifs (fish, birds, animals, solar and lunar symbols, plant meanders) does not appear to relate to other Lampung textiles. Late 19th or early 20th century; 82 x 91.5 cm. Collection: Rubinstein.*

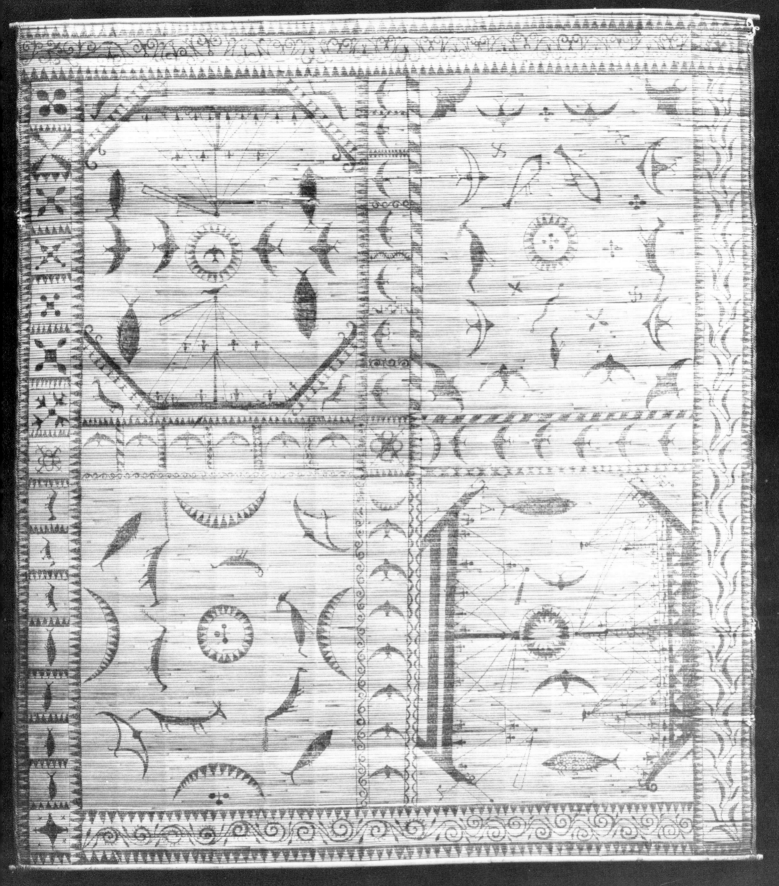

12

Fig. 14: *Major pictorial mats from Timor are little known, but important in their own right. A giant horned lizard with bifurcated tail is the main focus of this Atoni example. Within and around him are more lizards, anthropomorphs, and snakes in an intricate interlocking mass of positive and negative forms. The design concept of figures containing and surrounded by other figures, often with common heads or body parts, is also found in Atoni textiles. In some instances in Indonesia, mythical ancestors are said to have been born as crocodiles or lizards. Pre-WWII; 174 x 53 cm. Private collection.*

Fig. 17: *The seat- or buttocks-mat, once worn by men in several areas of Borneo, Sulawesi, and Maluku, represents a transition between mats and clothing. Attached by a cord around the waist and usually worn in combination with a loin cloth, it was both practical and provided a vehicle for fine decoration. This example from Kaliman tan is plaited of black rotan with a pattern layer of natural rotan on top and a carefu ly applied display of cut-out commercial cotton, minute beads, buttons, a shell disk, and long tassels. The beads are strung on bast fiber as separate, shaped pieces and thei secured to the mat. The beadwork may have been done by the Maloh people, among whom motifs such as the displayed figure serve a guardian function. Pre-WWII; 51.5 x 25 cm. Private collection.*

Fig. 13: Plaited in black on natural split bamboo(?), this Lampung mat presents a very graphic design. It appears to have some similarities to the "red ship style" palepai (fig. 47), although there is only one large ship rather than two, and small ships on either side instead. The hooked projections that define the two ends of the red ships in the palepai have in this mat expanded to occupy the whole deck, leaving room for only one architectural element to be placed there instead of three. A most unusual feature are the dentates that project from each of the hooks, perhaps representing growth forms or tendrils. Mats like this were probably used for wall display. Collection: Anita E. Spertus and Robert J. Holmgren, New York.

placed under the corpse during the washing. The use of patterned *lampit* apparently occurs in few areas—the Krui coast and around Semangka Bay.[37] The ship motifs found on some of these *lampit* may be symbolic vehicles for use during rites of passage; the significance of the other motifs—birds, sun and moon, plants, fish—is not clear.

Also from Sumatra, from the Lampung region, come some particularly graphic mats. Their motifs, in black and sometimes red split bamboo on a natural background, include large ship forms, trees, animals, birds, and anthropomorphic figures (fig. 13); they immediately recall the forms and motifs of *palepai* and *tampan*, the long and the square woven forms of ceremonial "ship cloths" from the same area. The only places indicated for their manufacture are Katimbang in the far south of the Kalianda peninsula and the Anyer-Kidul area in West Java, settled by Lampung immigrants. Some were used as sitting mats and others as wall hangings on festive occasions. Some may have been part of a bride's trousseau.[38]

While the Sumatran and Borneo mats described above have received some documentation, those from Timor have received very little. Both the Atoni (fig. 14) and the Tetum peoples (fig. 15) make bold figural mats that also appear to bear a close relationship to textile motifs and are sophisticated forms that could have emerged from only well-established traditions.

In considering fabric traditions, it is instructive to examine some crossover points between mats and other plaitwork on one hand, and woven textiles on the other. The term "plaitwork" is used here to describe mats, hats, baskets, etc. that use the technique loosely described as plaiting and employ materials that are relatively inflexible and result in fabrics of little pliability. They are contrasted to cloth, which has no inherent rigid or inflexible elements.

Sometimes plaitwork patterns appear to have been transferred directly to textiles, a process that probably has been continuing for centuries. In each case, however, it is difficult to prove that patterns did not transfer the other way. Among the reliefs on the main Shiva temple of Prambanan, consecrated in A.D. 856, is a house with a plaitwork shutter.[39] The square over-under nature of the pattern is clearly visible and is imitated in the modern batik motif *anyam tikar*. Plaitwork motifs like the eight-pointed star (fig. 16) are shared by many textiles, some of which recreate it in a similar weaving structure, others in dye. Some details of plaitwork that are determined by the technique itself are apparently imitated in other techniques, for no obvious reason. In several ikat traditions, for example, the bodies of figures are filled with small squares or dots, similar to those in simple diagonal plaitwork. Sometimes complete patterns are transferred to another medium or technique, probably because the significance of the motifs is the same in each.

Another crossover point is in the use of plaitwork for clothing. Such use is documented for Indonesia's distant historical and cultural neighbors, such as Madagascar, where shirts of matting were made,[40] and Micronesia, where mat skirts have been used as clothing into the present century.[41] But there is little evidence of such clothing worn by people in Indonesia, although palm leaf and pandanus plaitwork garments were used by the women of the Aru Islands.[42] The seat-mat is an item that suggests an interim step: it is worn, but is also used as a mat (fig. 17).

Some techniques are applied to both plaitwork and textiles. In the seat-mat, for example, appliqué work has been used on a plaitwork foundation. This comfortable blend of plaitwork and textile techniques is found in important objects such as the Sumba man's betel

Fig. 16: A villager sits in front of the plaited, split bamboo wall of a Flores house. As a permanent architectural component, the wall demonstrates the versatility of plaitwork in scale and use. Plaitwork such as this has inspired many textile designs, and the eight-pointed star is rendered in many techniques across the Archipelago. (For a discussion of plaitwork see Emery, The Primary Structures of Fabrics, p. 68.) Field photograph, Menno van Wyk, 1977.

bag where straightforward plaitwork (fig. 18) is elaborated with, for example, fine needlework (fig. 19).

Further links between plaitwork and textiles are seen in the three-dimensional hexagonal plaitwork found in several islands. In the Lesser Sundas, special baskets for serving food or storing valuables are made with carefully constructed, three-dimensional figures on the lids (fig. 20). These "sculpted" motifs also appear on textiles, sharing the same cultural sources and significance. Three-dimensional plaitwork is found also in the form of effigy figures. Some of these are associated with offerings related to the agricultural cycle. In Bali, at the beginning of every harvest, the image of the Rice Mother, *nini pantun,* is made from harvested rice stalks and then decorated.[43] Related to her are small images of plaited lontar leaves with fan-shaped or rayed headdresses. These figures are generally referred to as *cili.* They are symbols of wealth, fertility and good luck, and are dedicated to the rice goddess Dewi Sri who, in the process of the Hinduization of Bali, tended to take the place of the more archaic Rice Mother.[44] The *cili* motif is found widely in Bali, in particular on the *lamak,* ephemeral long panels made of cutout and pinned coconut leaves that hang before altars and shrines. For every festival they are made anew, except on the rare occasions when a woven textile is used as a substitute.[45] Various techniques appear to have been used in these woven *lamak*—the rare supplementary warp,[46] weft ikat (fig. 21), and supplementary weft.

Fig. 18: Even this Sumbanese man's basic betel bag has essential ritual roles, for example, in courtship play or as a repository for his spirit—perhaps in the manner that the sacred keris *(heirloom dagger) is an extension of a man's persona. Height: 14 x 18.5 cm. Collection: van Wyk and Warren.*

Fig. 19: This Sumba betel bag represents a sophisticated evolutionary step beyond the bag in fig. 18. Black embroidery thread has been needleworked into the natural-colored plaitwork surface—a technique more usually applied to textiles. Height: 19 x 26.5 cm. Collection: Bierlich.

Fig. 20: The rooster finial atop this tiered basket from East Sumba represents a three-dimensional plaitwork tradition. All the components of the lid, including the three hexagonal tiers with detailed flower buds, leaves and the crowning bird, were constructed as a single unit—a commanding feat in both conception and execution. The rooster is a prominent Sumbanese motif and perhaps reflects the use of the chicken for augury and ritual sacrifice. The red rooster is also a magically powerful presence in funerary rites. Height: 21.5 cm. Collection: van Wyk and Warren.

Fig. 15: A dramatic display of figured mats of lontar palm leaves is suspended beneath the roof overhang to shade the outer porch of a Timor house in the Tetum village of Failuka. The patterns and colors apparently identify social relations in the community, as well as the marital status of females in the household. The bold, polychrome designs are common to textiles over a large area of Indonesia. Most notable is the mat on the far left that presents a clear example of interlocking tiers of anthropomorphic figures, a pan-Southeast Asian design. Field photograph, Laurence A. G. Moss, 1982.

Fig. 21: The frontal figure of this weft ikat has a headdress, large earrings, and prominent hands that suggest the form of a cili, *which the Balinese generally associate with Dewi Sri, the goddess of rice and agricultural fertility. The form is commonly found in* lamak, *altar decorations or banners of cut palm leaves which have been freshly plaited and pinned. They are hung in quantity in temples and on shrines for festivals. This cloth may be a woven substitute for a* lamak *that could be used over and over rather than newly made each time. Warp 70.5 cm, weft 70 cm. Collection: Museum of Cultural History, UCLA.*

Fig. 22: This beaded, fringed apron, sassang, is part of the costume that Sa'dan Toraja women wear for the Ma'gellu' dance, performed at the feast concluding the death rites for a person of noble rank. Suspended from a tablet-woven belt, the glass beads, predominantly yellow (considered a color of heavenly origin), are strung in an open network, forming a repeating geometric motif that contains small snakes, similar to those in the panels of Toraja houses. Belt: warp 118 cm, weft 3.5 cm. Beads: 34.5 cm long, 56 cm wide. Private collection.

Beads and Shells:
Echoes of an Ancient Trade

Small and portable, imperishable, and infinitely varied, the beads found in Indonesia have passed through many hands. Both locally made and imported beads have been used for thousands of years. Archaeological evidence from a Timor site, for example, dates beads to approximately 3000 B.C.[47] Over the centuries, beads, primarily glass and stone, from Europe, the Middle East, India, and China were carried to the Archipelago where, as popular trade items, they worked their way into the most remote areas. Each society or group found value in different types of beads and created a local terminology and lore around them. In some places beads became treasured heirlooms or items of wealth and prestige, some even supplied with a divine origin.

With a few exceptions, such as the use of large beads in the Kelabit woman's cap,[48] the smaller and medium-sized glass beads were used in fabric items. Sometimes the beads were strung in an open network, on various supporting fibers, and shaped into structures such as beaded collars, or long "tunics" such as those found among the Western Toraja[49] and the Iban.[50] The addition of long fringes, hanging heavily because of the cumulative weight of the beads, but moving in unison when the wearer followed the steps of a dance or procession, must have been effective. The Sa'dan Toraja of southwestern Sulawesi excelled at this kind of beadwork, as is seen in their beaded aprons, *sassang*, supported only from a narrow waistband (fig. 22), and their beaded hangings, *kandaure*. Both carry schematic motifs similar to those carved on wooden panels on Toraja houses that express wishes for safety, prosperity, and long life.

When beads were used for garments, they were more often applied to a backing or support material. In some instances, beads were made into separate network panels or strips that could be removed from one surface when it wore out and applied to another. In other cases they were secured individually or in strands to the support material. In many islands we find headbands, hats, belts, baskets, bags, and boxes on which beads have been applied with infinite patience and skill to a plaitwork backing, or skirts and jackets where beads are applied to cloth or bark-cloth. The Ngada of Flores, for example, applied beads to the indigo tube skirts of their noblewomen (fig. 23). The somber blue warp ikat patterns in narrow warp stripes are overlaid with solid networks and loose strands of bright beads applied with little regard for the underlying pattern. These skirts are a striking and noteworthy example of Indonesian beadwork.

In the Lampung region of South Sumatra, several types of ceremonial objects were once made of beads. The rare beaded squares (called *tampan maju*)[51] and the long forms (fig. 24)[52] (loosely referred to as "beaded *palepai*" because of their resemblance to the long woven *palepai* of the region) are of artistic, technical, and historical interest. The *tampan maju* were probably given and displayed at wedding ceremonies,[53] while the beaded *palepai* were probably made to be hung as a prestige wall display, although occasions for their use are not documented. Because of the weight of the beads, both of these fabrics have a sturdy plaitwork foundation, sometimes covered with cloth, to which the strands of beads are applied. There appear to be two styles of application: in one, short strands of beads are couched (and sometimes stitched directly?) to the backing, in any free-form direction desired, packed densely, so that the beads present a solid face (panels with animals and riders in particular seem to be executed in this manner); in the other, the bead strands are more widely spaced so that the backing is visible, and the patterns tend to be more geometric. So few of these beaded pieces are known that it is difficult to form an adequate picture of the range of motifs that might have existed, yet it is clear that they are among the most significant pieces of beadwork in the Archipelago.

In some beaded *tampan* and *palepai,* beads are complemented by borders of small white nassa shells and occasionally cowries. The nassa shells were ground down and a hole was drilled or punched in them so they could be applied flat to whatever fabric was used. Sometimes the shells are the principal patterning material, as in some skirts and jackets of the Maloh people in western Kalimantan (fig. 25; fig. 26).[54] When used alone on a contrasting ground, they can have a particularly dramatic effect.

Fig. 23: A beadwork ship, figures, and other motifs that may represent animals and celestial symbols are applied to the lower part of a tube skirt (lawo butu) from west central Flores. Ngada women of the highest social rank still make fine deeply saturated, indigo-dyed, warp ikat skirts with stick-like motifs such as horses. However, the beadwork and use of the dye Morinda citrifolia to create the brown stripes seen in this example were probably discontinued in the 1920's when the area was partly Christianized.

The beads are strung on multistranded cotton yarn and anchored to the skirt, in some areas rather casually. As is true of all such skirts, whole or partial motifs could have been recycled from another skirt. It is also possible that minor parts of the beadwork could have been added at different times, even quite recently by dealers. Although the significance of the motifs is no longer remembered, these garments may still be worn for ceremonial dancing during part of the agricultural cycle and are tied at a woman's shoulders by embroidered cotton loops at the top selvage. (See R. J. Maxwell, "Ceremonial Textiles of the Ngada of Eastern Indonesia.") Warp 178 cm, weft 177 cm. Collection: Manring.

23

24

25

26

Fig. 24: Dense beadwork applied to long plaitwork mats appears to be a very rare form. These mats are sometimes referred to as "beaded palepai" and occur only in South Sumatra. Beads cover the entire surface of the mat and are strung on thick cotton and secured at intervals. Although they appear to be made to hang for display purposes, little is known about the use of "beaded palepai." This example is subdivided into seven sections, each filled with a different animal, including an elephant, a water snake, a deer, and a horse with a rider, and executed in a confident curvilinear style. Late 19th or early 20th century; 231 x 20 cm. Collection: Manring.

Fig. 25: Beads and shells elaborate the ceremonial costumes of several groups of people of western Kalimantan who do not generally weave. They obtain cloth, beads, and shells in trade from their neighbors. This woman's skirt (kain buri) from the Maloh people has coarse black or blue cloth used as a foundation that contrasts powerfully with the white tendril-like motifs of the nassa shellwork. It is also decorated with beads and slit bells. Warp 96 cm, weft 59 cm. Collection: Manring.

Fig. 26: A naga or snake-like motif outlined in nassa shells dominates back and front of this man's vest from the Maloh people of western Kalimantan. In Borneo such curvilinear motifs are sometimes called aso. The vest (sapé buri) is trimmed in cloth, felt, beads, sequins, bronze ornaments, and coins marked "C. V. Brooke, Rajah, Sarawak." It is lined with old pieces of pua kumbu, probably obtained from the Iban. 56 x 42 cm. Collection: Moss.

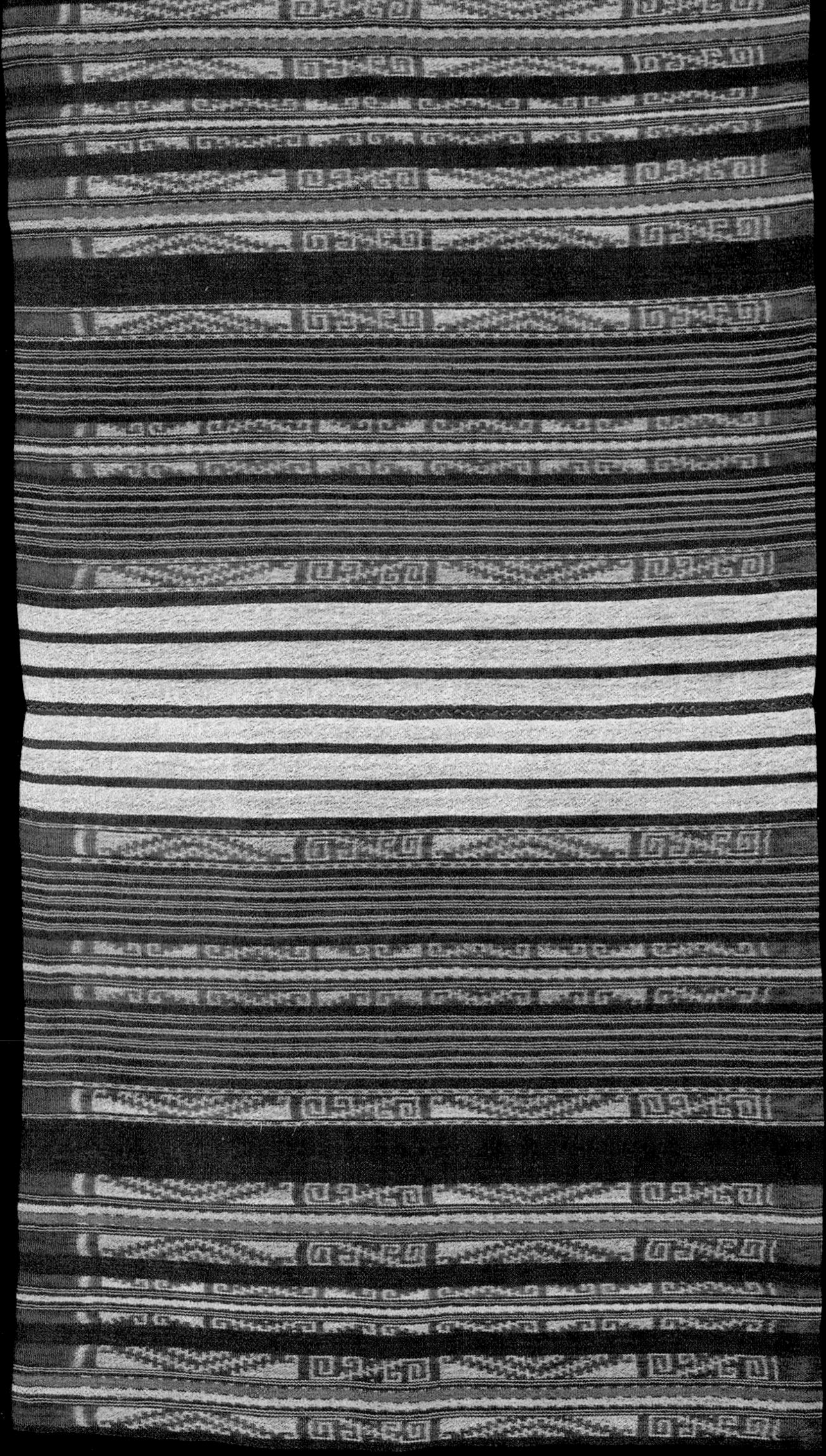

Warp Stripes and Warp Ikat

One of the simplest methods of patterning a textile is by the use of different colored warp yarns grouped to form longitudinal stripes. Different colored wefts can also be used in the weaving process to create weft bands and, if woven into a striped warp, to create a plaid or a check. Such simple striped or plaid fabrics are found throughout the Archipelago, mostly as everyday wear. Yet certain striped cloths are traditionally considered sacred and imbued with magical powers. To make these cloths the weaver must fulfill such rituals as fasting, avoidance of certain foods, the making of offerings, or the restriction of weaving to specified times or days. For example, in Lombok, a sacred cloth, *umbaq kombong,* with warp stripes of varying widths is woven under ritual conditions for use in life-cycle ceremonies such as haircutting and circumcision.[55]

It is not difficult to imagine the weaving of striped fabrics in which some or all of the yarns for the warp stripes have undergone a further patterning process before they come to the loom, or to imagine that this process, warp ikat, would also involve ritual requirements, especially for fabrics having ritual purposes.

In Indonesia, warp ikat patterning is done mostly on cotton, occasionally on bast or leaf fibers, rarely on silk. It occurs in many areas of the Archipelago. We find, even today, a great variety of ritual requirements associated with spinning and binding the yarns, gathering the dye materials, preparing the dye, immersing the yarns, and cutting the warps after weaving. For example, the weaver may not be menstruating, she may fast, begin on an auspicious day, make a ceremonial offering of food, place apotropaic objects around the dye pots, recite special prayers, and so on. Dyeing may be done in a secret place, and the presence of men may not be tolerated. Particular dye recipes may be carefully preserved and handed down among only a privileged few—often dyeing is the prerogative of women from the highest class in a society—or particular ingredients may be added to the dye vats for their magical as well as practical significance. The value placed on dyeing and preparing yarn is frequently reflected in the carefully, sometimes elaborately, made tools and equipment: decorated dye pots, carved tying frames and thread winders, spinning wheels, etc.

The simplest warp ikat patterns are squares, triangles, arrows, and uncomplicated geometric forms, in one color, placed in a few narrow stripes in an otherwise plain textile. Indeed it is possible to argue that textiles patterned with plain warp stripes of different colors interspersed with a few ikat-patterned warps demonstrate the most archaic applications of the technique. There have been no archaeological discoveries of old ikats in Indonesia. There are, however, two ikat fragments from a burial cave in Banton Island, east of Mindoro in the Philippines, that offer tantalizing possibilities. Once wrapped around a corpse and placed in a wooden coffin, they are dated, apparently by association with other artifacts, to the fourteenth century. They appear to be bast or leaf fiber with unpatterned natural and red-brown stripes alternating with blue and white ikat-patterned stripes.[56] The ikat motifs are the simple geometric forms noted above together with an elementary bird figure. Even if the proposed date is two hundred years too early, they would still be the earliest known ikats in island Southeast Asia and would give tentative support to the notion that some of the most archaic ikats are of this kind—a kind still found today in eastern Indonesia, for example in Tanimbar (fig. 27).

West of Tanimbar, ikats are made with a few wider stripes. Kisar tube skirts include one slightly wider ikat-patterned stripe in each panel (fig. 28) which contains a pictorial motif—

Fig. 29: Lizards (or crocodiles?), birds, and hooks with emerging anthropomorphic figures enliven the narrow, blue and white warp ikat bands of this man's cloth (selimut) from the Atoni of western Timor. Each patterned band highlights the center of a polychrome, warp-striped panel. Three panels make up the cloth. Pre-WWII; warp 212 cm, weft 107 cm. Collection: Moss.

Fig. 30: Human figures and birds are mirror-imaged where the two panels of this tube skirt are joined. Made by Atoni women in the Oinlasi area of western Timor, such skirts are little seen today, although some women still wear them under other garments. Warp 134 cm, weft 118 cm. Collection: Moss.

29

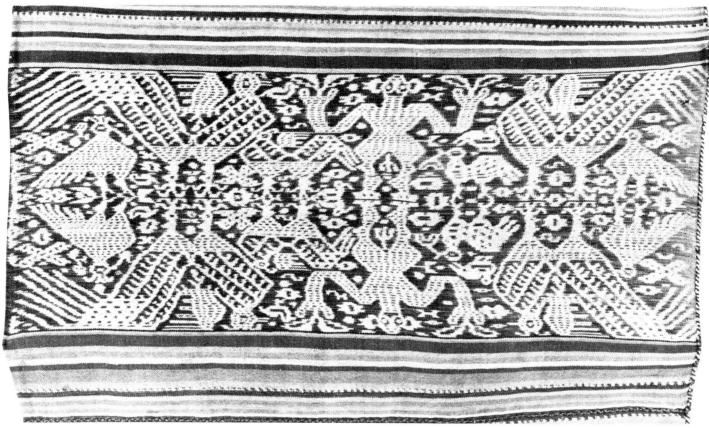

30

32

humans with arms raised, mounted figures, and birds. Similar motifs appear within the blue and white ikat stripes of garments made by the Atoni women in Timor. While some of the stripes are narrow and favor long-tailed lizards and hook-and-lozenge motifs that suggest abstracted anthropomorphic forms (fig. 29), other stripes have become more dominant. Sometimes this is achieved by mirror-imaging, which doubles the power of the figures by repetition (fig. 30), or by widening the stripe still further until the figures become massive giants (fig. 31). Widening the stripe, giving the figures greater visual prominence and potentially greater magical power, may be a later evolutionary step.

The Tetum of Central Timor (also referred to as Belu by their Atoni neighbors) have responded to the boundaries imposed by the retention of warp stripes in their textiles by making subtle two-color ikats with a disciplined technical excellence. Especially in the men's sashes and the ceremonial cloths (fig. 32), there is a main pattern stripe surrounded by many very narrow patterned stripes that create the effect of total surface coverage, even though there are plain warps between them.

Fig. 31: Monumental anthropomorphic figures, surrounded by birds and smaller figures, occupy the entire width of the center panel of a man's shoulder or waist cloth (selimut), from the Atoni of western Timor. These wide stripes of warp ikat seem to be a development from earlier, narrower stripes. In this case the figures lie across the direction of the warp, but sometimes figures are made even larger by orienting them along the warp. Pre-WWII; warp 210 cm, weft 43 cm. Collection: Moss.

Fig. 32: This rare textile was once used as a cloth for special ceremonies such as the occupation of a new house, the wrapping of a body at funerary rites, and the decoration of horses, possibly at certain death ceremonies. Made by Tetum people in the village of Kaletek, in the South Belu area of Central Timor, and estimated by them to be over 100 years old, this cloth is believed to contain motifs so powerful that the living might not speak of them to strangers. The largest motif, locally called marobo, may represent a human figure, but the predominantly schematic motifs remain unexplained. There is no doubt, however, that the absolutely precise workmanship in ikat, saturated dyeing, weaving, and finishing represents the most sophisticated development of the archaic textile form of warp ikat between plain stripes. Pre-1911; warp 219 cm, weft 122 cm. Collection: Moss.

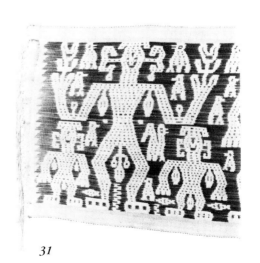

31

Fig. 33: After the harvest, young Suwanese men and women have an opportunity to meet and perhaps begin the courting process. Wearing plaited square rattle-baskets tied to their ankles, they move together with other villagers in the cadence of a nighttime dance, their warp ikat garments a chain of shifting patterns. It is only when such textiles are worn with the unconscious grace of those for whom they are made that the true aesthetic of Indonesian textiles finds expression. Photographed in a small village near Seba, Sawu, by Laurence A. G. Moss, 1981.

Textiles from the islands north and west of Timor show further local versions of the placement of warp ikat stripes between plain stripes. In Sawu, where textile motifs for ceremonial cloths have remained conservative (fig. 33), men's shoulder cloths have an uneven number of narrow warp ikat stripes with alternating small motifs. Together with specific dye colors, these motifs identify the wearer's membership in the Greater or Lesser Blossom group, a social division determined by the affinity of the wearer's mother and maintained for the proper arrangement of marriages and other life-cycle ceremonies. Lacking such ritual restrictions, cloths for everyday wear carry more freely chosen motifs. In the women's skirts, these motifs appear in the widest stripe in both panels (fig. 34; fig. 35).

The women of Lembata Island make long ceremonial tube skirts in which the width of the ikat stripes varies. The more important the cloth, the more and wider the stripes. When the panels (sometimes five or more) are sewn together, the widest (considered the most important) is in the center.[57] The motifs in the stripes range from geometric forms, such as linked chains of anthropomorphic figures, to naturalistic birds and animals.

The surface of the tube skirts from Lio, Flores are typically covered with a network of fine lines from which emerge attenuated forms—human, animal, and floral-geometric figures, framed in small rectangles. Only a few plain warp stripes are to be found, in the top and bottom panels. In other Flores ikats, however, the notion of warp ikat bounded by plain warp stripes disappears altogether when figural representation and local motifs give way to those inspired by *patola* cloth from India.

Indeed, the most important factor affecting the arrangement and character of many Indonesian textiles, including warp ikats, has been the centuries-old trade in Indian cloths, particularly the double ikat silk *patola* of Gujarat. These textiles generally became the valued possessions of the nobility or upper classes. Because of their rarity and the mystery associated with their creation (double ikat is unknown in most of Indonesia), they were revered as heirlooms and occasionally regarded as embodying magical powers. Both their individual motifs and their spatial arrangement—large centerfield with side borders and end panels including *tumpal* motifs—were incorporated into many Indonesian textiles.[58]

In eastern Indonesia, *patola* was very important in Roti. From the mid-seventeenth century the local rulers allied themselves in trade agreements with the Dutch, who provided muskets, gin, and royal regalia, including *patola,* in return for slaves, wax, and foodstuffs.[59] Some older forms of textiles from Roti and the neighboring island of Ndao maintain a warp ikat pattern arrangement within warp stripes, but more often today both men's cloths and

Fig. 34: *This suggestion of a human form with arms raised, emerging from the branches of a tree, is an example of a characteristic sometimes encountered in Indonesian textiles where one form is rendered in a way that suggests another. This detail comes from one of the widest warp ikat stripes in a tube skirt from Sawu. Warp 120 cm, weft 170.5 cm. Collection: Moss.*

Fig. 35: *The main motifs in the widest stripes of everyday Sawunese tube skirts are inspired by many sources. This abstract form appears to be a piece of traditional heirloom jewelry. Warp 123 cm, weft 171 cm. Collection: Manring.*

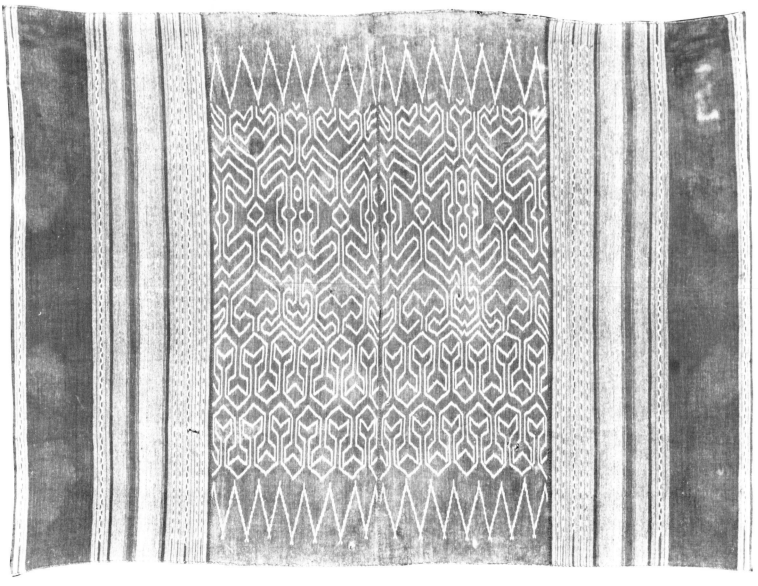

Fig. 36: *The gray-brown, warp ikat center panel of this shroud, possibly from the To Mangi Toraja people, may have been dyed by immersion in mud. The spaces between the clear white resisted lines are precisely proportioned so that light and dark are exactly balanced. From the schematic matrix emerge what appear to be lizards with tiers of interlocked anthropomorphic figures on either side of them. Pre-WWII; warp 138 cm, weft 188 cm. Collection: Grace.*

women's tube skirts have the larger pattern fields with side borders. *Patola* motifs, particularly the eight-pointed flower in circular or square repeats, are reserved for the nobility while commoners may wear simpler floral or local motifs.

It may not have been the influence of *patola* alone that led to the development of large centerfield designs in warp ikats. The use of plain warp stripes between the ikat portions was one way of making patterned warps, which took time to prepare, go farther. In cloths for important occasions, a greater proportion of ikat patterning was perhaps a reflection of their special value. This may be true of the Toraja warp ikats from southwestern Sulawesi, which bear little resemblance to archaic forms of warp ikat from elsewhere on the island that carried modest patterns between plain warp stripes. These southwestern Toraja ikats are grand in both scale and design concept. Used as shrouds where they were made in the isolated valleys around Rongkong and Galumpang, the ikats were traded to other Toraja who also used them as ceremonial hangings and canopies.[60] Some pieces were used in the form of long panels, sometimes exceeding twelve feet in length. Other pieces were cut and sewn into a rectangular form three or four panels wide. Even when warp ikat stripes alternate with plain stripes in an almost equal balance, the power and scale of the ikat motifs is apparent. In other shrouds, the center is often entirely ikat, with plain stripes in the side panels (fig. 36). This format provides a large centerfield in which the angular interlocking geometric forms that dominate much Toraja design are most dramatically displayed. The people themselves apparently no longer remember the full significance of their patterns. A number of the designs are versions of that pan-Indonesian pattern that is described as tiers and rows of anthropomorphic figures, sometimes sharing common heads. Perhaps representing ancestors, these figures are not inappropriate for shrouds.[61] When the limits of warp stripes are transcended, as occurs on the Atoni warp ikats with their giant figures and the Toraja ikats with large centerfields, a major shift in design concept and potential occurs; this shift has produced some of the most powerful and dramatic imagery in all Indonesian textiles.

Particularly dramatic are the *pua kumbu,* the sacred blanket-sized textiles made by the Borneo Iban. With almost all the available surface used for warp ikat, the centerfield usually consists of several side-by-side repeats of a pattern extending from top to bottom of the cloth. The Iban predilection for detail sometimes finds expression in masses of tendrils and small animals and insects embedded in the design, but the major motifs still emerge strongly in the most outstanding pieces.

Whereas narrow selvage stripes or panels are still retained on Iban *pua,* they are not found on the majority of Sumba warp ikats. Generally, the patterns of these cloths are placed in

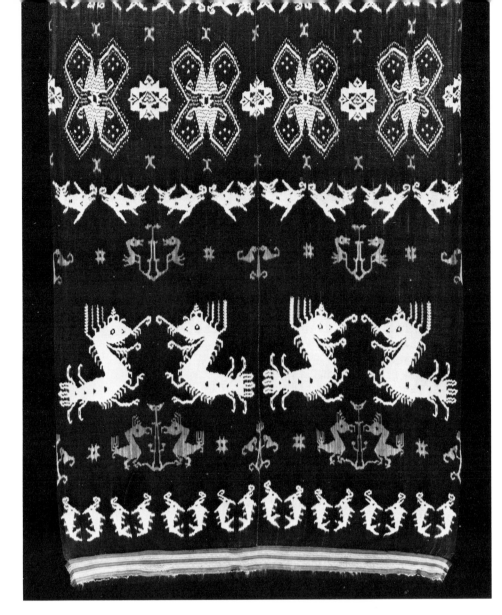

Fig. 37: This blue, warp ikat, man's cloth (hinggi kawuru) from East Sumba has bands of confronting animals—seahorses, dolphins, fish, crowned shrimp, and cockatoos. Warp 157 cm, weft 113 cm. Collection: Moss.

Fig. 38: A retainer of the late Raja of Pau, East Sumba, models the prestigious gold headdress (lamba) with its diamond-shaped pendants (mamuli), the gold neck chain (kanataru), and disk (kawadaku) that complement the pair of hinggi cloths worn across the shoulder and around the waist for ceremonial occasions. Here only the waist cloth is worn. Both lamba and mamuli occur as textile motifs. Field photograph, Menno van Wyk, 1977.

Fig. 39: Seated at her tying frame, a woman from the family of the Raja of Rende in Sumba ties stretched warp yarns into groups that will form a "skull tree" motif on a hinggi. Field photograph, Laurence A. G. Moss, 1979.

38

horizontal bands of varying widths, an arrangement unique to Sumba (fig. 37). The men's ikat textiles, *hinggi,* once reserved for noble families and their retainers (fig. 38), were worn for ritual events and were an essential component of the bridewealth exchange and of the funerary gifts for important persons.[62] Rows of trees, birds, animals, and sea creatures from the Sumbanese environment, together with skull trees (fig. 39) and a few introduced figures such as rampant lions borrowed from Dutch heraldic designs, figure in more conventional *hinggi.* In some, a center band contains special symbols identifying particular noble families. With their fine balance and vitality, the best examples of *hinggi* constitute some of the most strongly pictorial textiles in Indonesia.

39

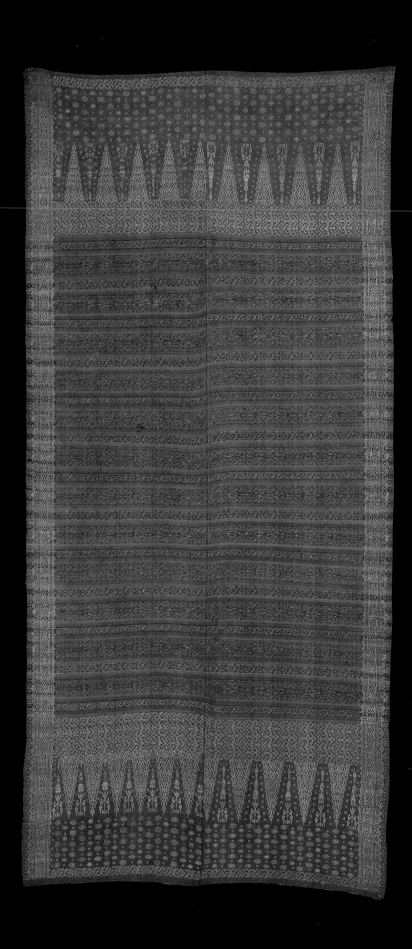

Exotic Silks and International Trade

The annals of the Liang dynasty (A.D. 502-557) record that in the kingdom of P'o-li: "The king uses a texture [sic] of flowered silk wrapped round his body; on his head he wears a golden hat of more than one foot high . . . adorned with various precious stones."[63] Professor O. Wolters has theorized that P'o-li was in East Java.[64] If so, this passage establishes that at least three centuries before the great temples had been built in Central Java and the jeweled figures and richly patterned textiles had been carved on their stone walls, kingly garments made of silk were already luxury items in the Javanese courts. There appears to have been little commerce on the sea route between China and Indonesia until the early fifth century A.D. when the southern Chinese dynasties began to trade with Southeast Asia to obtain forest resins and other products that had formerly come overland from western Asia. Southeast Asian merchants were the intermediaries, and the currency of the trade was Chinese silk, which by then was also in demand for the Persian and the Indian markets.[65] Western Indonesians are thought to have sailed to India and Ceylon by this time and, between 430 and 473, they sent twenty tribute missions to China from the several kingdoms of Java and Sumatra.[66] Tributes were sent irregularly for several centuries, an elaborate guise for continuing trade relations. Silks figured prominently in the gifts exchanged, and perhaps the envoys brought back silkworms. The annals of the Sung dynasty (A. D. 960-1279) describe the inhabitants of one of the Javanese kingdoms: "The people are also engaged in rearing silkworms and making silk; they weave a thin silk, a yellow silk and a cloth made of cotton."[67] Thus, silk was made locally in Indonesia as well as imported, a situation still true today.

From the mid-seventh century when the Sumatran kingdom of Srivijaya consolidated its hegemony over western Indonesia, maritime trade with western Asia brought Indians, Arabs, and Persians, who, like the Chinese, sought not only Indonesian native products, including camphor and spices, but also each other's textiles. The ports on the straits of Malacca were transhipment points, and the effects of this trade were felt throughout the Archipelago. During this time also, Islam began its steady spread, and numerous Indian cloths—plain, stamped, striped, and plaid, but particularly the prized *patola* silk—became much in demand. When the Portuguese and later the Dutch arrived, they built their trading networks on established foundations. The first four Dutch ships to reach Indonesia came to Bantam in West Java in 1596 and encountered a polyglot trading community. The Chinese were observed to bring "all sorts of silk woven and unwoven, twined and untwined."[68] With the unprecedented success of their first sale of Chinese silk in Amsterdam in 1604, the Dutch became deeply involved in the manipulation of Chinese, Indian, and Persian silk supplies to meet fluctuating demands from Amsterdam. Throughout the seventeenth century, the logistics of this operation were controlled from Batavia, (now Jakarta). The Dutch also operated textile factories in India to supply the Indies market with cottons and silks in return for pepper, spices, sugar, coffee, tea, etc.[69] Wherever the Dutch made trade agreements with local rulers, textiles, particularly *patola,* were included in the arrangements. Thus the traffic in silks has always been exotic and complex, both India and China serving as suppliers for the Indonesian market.

The greatest variety and elaboration of silks are found in Sumatra, probably because of its position in the old trading world. Today, silks are usually part of ritual costume or hung as rich displays for ceremonial occasions. They are medium-to-light in weight and dyed predominantly in the red-blue range of the spectrum, in intense tones enhanced by the reflective characteristics of the silk itself. Weft ikat and supplementary weft with metallic yarns are the patterning techniques of choice, with some *plangi.* Silk weft ikat has particular subtleties of color where the dyes have wicked, or bled, slightly under the resist bindings, leaving soft edges to the patterns. Metallic yarns provide the brilliance and texture essential to a grand display. There is sometimes an undercurrent of Islam-influenced forms, seen in the occasional use of plaid grounds instead of weft ikat and in the preference for fine floral and geometric motifs. The pattern repeats are relatively small, the effect of the textiles coming not from vivid and dramatic imagery but from the cumulation of smaller, brilliant units. Palembang silks epitomize these characteristics to the greatest degree, while other areas have their own substyles. Silks from the Pasemah region in the southwestern highlands, for example, lean toward brown tones, occasionally including an animal or human figure motif that is recognizably related to the textiles of the Lampung region. These pieces are narrower than those found in Palembang, and two lengths are sewn together to make a skirt cloth (fig. 40). In the western region, the Minangkabau use supplementary weft metallic yarns to

Fig. 40 (left): Usually identified as coming from Pasemah, west of Palembang in South Sumatra, these shoulder or skirt cloths employ a range of soft red-brown tones in alternating plain and weft ikat stripes, sometimes framed by supplementary weft in metallic yarns. Here two narrow panels are seamed to form a skirt cloth, of the kind worn by young men during bachelor dances. A most significant feature is the motif band just above the tumpal *end borders—a version of interlocking stylized human figures alternating in inverted and erect columns. Pre-WWII; warp 252 cm, weft 116 cm. Collection: Manring.*

produce textiles with densely packed surfaces (fig. 41). Sometimes they look more like metal than cloth. Possibly they also function as metal items in ritual gift exchanges.[70]

Silks are, or were, made in other areas of Indonesia, such as Java's North Coast, Sumbawa, and southern Sulawesi. The polychrome silks of Bali, worn as ceremonial costume, are particularly notable for the occasional, subtle use of silk rather than metallic supplementary wefts and for representation of *wayang* tableaux in polychrome weft ikat or in supplementary weft metallic yarns.

Fig. 41: The silks of the Minangkabau in West Sumatra sometimes have the finest, most densely woven, supplementary weft in the Archipelago. This woman's shawl or headdress from the Padang region is a little less lavish in its use of gold metallic yarn, so that the small check in the silk foundation is still visible. The end bands and fringes are given a special warmth by the addition of brightly colored silks that are worked between the metallic yarns. The bobbin lace trim at the ends was separately made, then attached after weaving. Warp 235 cm, weft 76.5 cm. Collection: van Wyk and Warren.

Of Ships and Trees:
Cotton Supplementary Weft Traditions

When supplementary weft techniques are used on a cotton, as opposed to silk foundation, the motifs seem to hark back to archaic or more local forms. These are seen, for example, in the geometric patterns in the end panels of some Batak shawls, shoulder cloths, and head cloths. Archetypal anthropomorphic forms and schematic motifs occur in Borneo textiles executed in the *pilih* technique, while plant forms are suggested by the repeating geometric motifs in small textiles from Lombok. From Sumbawa come motifs such as trees and ships with sails or banners aloft, crews of human figures, and birds in the rigging (fig. 42) that are immediately reminiscent of South Sumatran ship cloths. The latter are a large group of textiles in which the motifs are pictorial and in which ships and trees figure prominently. They provide some of the most universally intriguing images of all Indonesian textile art.

Fig. 42: The ship motif in the kepala *area of this cotton tube skirt from Sumbawa has hooked prows, a figure within a pavilion, and birds with high crests, curling wings and long tails. The motifs are derived from a design vocabulary very close to the ship cloths of South Sumatra. Even the rigid rows of very stylized figures above and below the ship are reminiscent of the rows of "crewmen" or "passengers" on some Sumatran cloths. Their single eye is said to be a sign that they are ancestors. The two-eyed fish in a row on the right of this detail resemble flat fish. If we borrow the Sumbanese belief that human souls invest themselves in such fish, this tableau might be seen as a representation of ancestral souls or spirits. Warp 189 cm, weft 119.5 cm. Collection: Manring.*

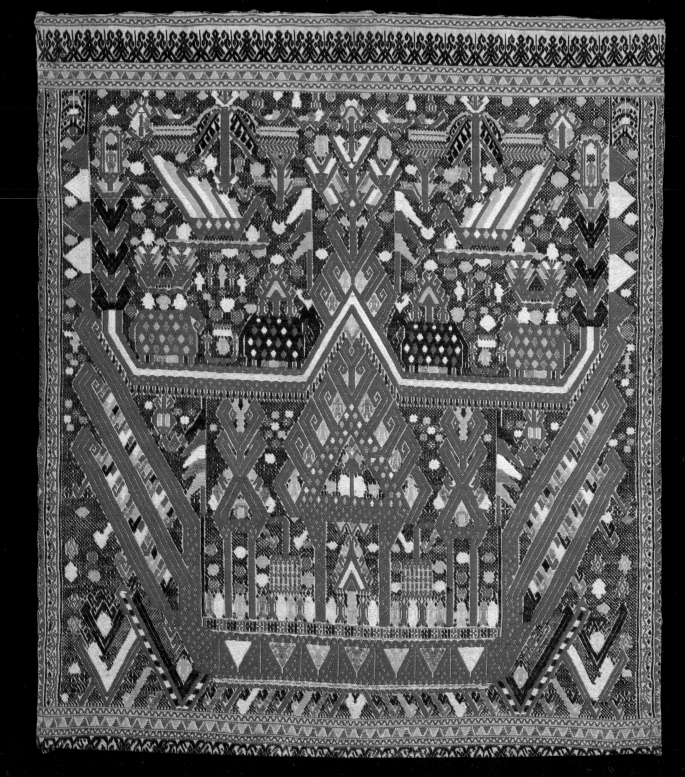

Fig. 43 (left): *The brilliant "red ship style" tampan from Kalianda in Sumatra is one of the most impressive of all ship cloths, in execution, color, and design. It is also one of the most important, as it appears to be the originating form for other ship cloths. This ship has steep, hooked prows and three buildings, possibly shrines, on its deck. There is also an upper level filled with processional animals, birds, trees, and small figures. It is possible to interpret this arrangement as a complex cosmological diagram representing a sacred realm. Late 19th or early 20th century; warp 97.5 cm (approx. 4 cm is missing on lower end), weft 82 cm. Collection: van Wyk and Warren.*

Fig. 46: *One group of tampan from the south coast of the Lampung region of Sumatra clearly represents events or commemorative scenes. Some of the occasions can be tentatively identified, such as a marriage or the birth of a noble child. Others, like this one, are more ambiguous. The central building has a tiered roof, probably not representing any architectural feature of the region, but perhaps an introduced element similar to a Javanese pavilion, pendapa. The peacocks and flags around the roof suggest an important occasion. Perhaps the figures that appear to be carrying boxes or bundles are bringing gifts or offerings to the central figure in the pavilion. The formal, confronting animals (lions or singa?) on either side of a stylized tree in the lower part, may be announcing the entrance to the upper realm above them. This hierarchical arrangement may be analagous to the gates and flanking animals at the foot of the tree depicted on the gunungan, the Javanese symbolic representation of the cosmic realm in which the wayang stories take place. Late 19th or early 20th century; warp 72 cm, weft 63 cm. Collection: Manring.*

Fig. 44: The central tree with spreading hooked branches that fill the cloth and provide a support for a host of creatures and figures is widely found in the Lampung region of Sumatra. Here the tree rises out of a flat, raft-like ship, the same form being inverted along the top, so that the two ships are like additional borders. In the laden branches are paired animals, with mounted riders, a variety of birds and several anthropomorphic figures. Some of the birds at the ends of the branches are upside down. While there is no specific interpretation available for this type of tree tampan, it may be regarded as a manifestation of a cosmic or world tree. In several Indonesian creation myths, the ancestral couple climbed down such a tree to the middle world of men, or moved out along its branches to experience great adventures and return with riches. Here silk is used for the supplementary weft. Late 19th or early 20th century; warp 98 cm, weft 85 cm. Collection: Leland.

"Ship cloth" is a convenient label for a Sumatran textile tradition that includes far more than ships.[71] These motifs were executed in the supplementary weft technique, generally in cotton, although silk was also used, and on a handspun, plain-woven cotton ground. Technical details of the weaving process and dyes used are a matter of conjecture, as the tradition lasted perhaps only until World War I. Three forms of cloth can be identified. The *tampan,* a small square, once the most widely used of the three, was distributed throughout the Lampung region and employed in a variety of situations through several levels of society. The *palepai,* a long cloth, was used as a ceremonial wall hanging by the upper classes in the south and southeast coastal areas and in a few inland areas, such as Jabung, to which coastal people migrated. The *tatibin,* a smaller long cloth, was apparently used in a manner parallel to some *palepai* and made only in a small southern coastal area between Semangka and Lampung bays.

In general terms, ship cloths were, and still may be, used at important life-cycle ceremonies, those associated, for example, with naming, haircutting, circumcision, marriage, building a new house, and death. The cloths' function seems to have been as a symbolic support that aided the individual during the transition from one life stage to the next. In addition, certain *palepai* would be hung in specific arrangements that represented the position of a family or clan within the social hierarchy. To some degree, the imagery on most ship cloths reflects these roles.

Tampan present the greatest range of imagery: true ship forms; ships that carry representations of architecture, trees, animals, and birds (fig. 43; fig. 44); and ships with other symbolic representations of animals and birds, such as hornbills paired with snakes (fig. 45). Some appear to be commemorating an event in a pictorial or narrative way, sometimes on board a ship, and sometimes with no ship present (fig. 46).[72] Some are more schematic and include, for example, stylized floral-geometric motifs or exaggerated large figures. The majority are executed in the continuous supplementary weft technique mostly in one major color.

Fig. 45: Sometimes a textile does not follow the expected form, and with the passage of years we may never know why. This piece appears to be a variation on the tampan *form, unusual for its rectangular instead of square shape, its* tumpal *end bands, and the presence of numerous mirror pieces applied to its surface. A complex set of large motifs such as this would normally occur only once on a* tampan; *here it occurs twice, in mirror image. Motifs represented here may be the archetypal agents of conflict between the earth and the heavens— the snake or* naga *versus the bird or hornbill. Although highly stylized, the lowest creature of the set has the characteristics of the hornbill as represented in other* tampan—*triangular protuberance between the legs, scroll or hook projections around the body, and protuberance from the bill. Above the hornbill are a pair of apparently joined or confronting snakes, each with diamond-shaped head and fangs. Between them rises a bipartite tree. Above this is an inverted flat-bottomed, simplified boat with its own inverted passengers, a* naga *with a monocular rider. Late 19th or early 20th century; warp 251 cm, weft 84 cm. Collection: Bierlich.*

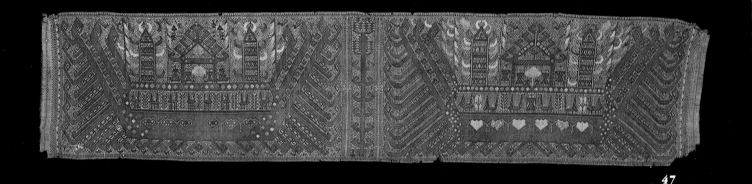

47

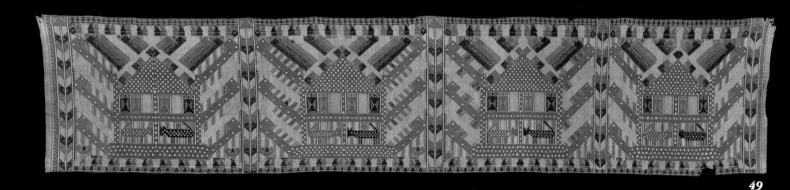

48

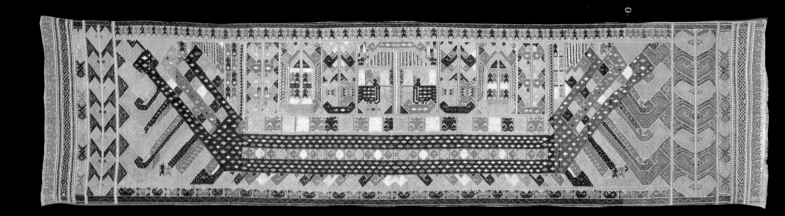

49

50

The introduction of the discontinuous supplementary weft technique, which permitted a number of color changes within the image, appears to be crucial in distinguishing *tampan* that are more likely to have come from the south or southeast coastal regions of Sumatra. From Kalianda, the peninsula in the far southeast Lampung region, come some particularly important *tampan*. They carry some of the most complex and sophisticated forms, executed in both continuous and discontinuous supplementary weft. Kalianda *tampan* of the "red ship style" are also considered the source of the Kalianda "red ship style" *palepai* (fig. 47) which is composed of two ships, side by side. The ships on both types of textile share high, hooked prows, hooks projecting from the hull, medallions on the hull itself, and three architectural elements, probably shrines, on deck. While the *tampan* has a clear upper level filled with animals, trees, and birds, in the *palepai* this level is represented by only a few small birds surrounding the shrines. Both the *tampan* and the *palepai* may be interpreted as a cosmic diagram.

In contrast, the "blue ship style" *palepai*, which originate more often from the Semangka Bay area, have ships with a steering oar and prows that are less steep (fig. 48). Usually a single ship rather than a pair occurs. The deck is divided into three main zones into which a variety of motifs are inserted—elements reflecting actual architecture, trees, confronting animals, etc.

One additional type of *palepai* that comes both from the Semangka Bay area and from Kalianda features rows of figures with no large ship at all. Although the number of rows may vary in individual cloths, the frontal figures all have horned heads, broad shoulders, and indefinite skirt and leg arrangements. Another style of *palepai*, in which motifs such as houses (fig. 49) or trees (fig. 50) are arranged in repeating panels, is of particular technical interest. The pieces from Kalianda are woven on a long warp with repeating designs already oriented in the horizontal fashion in which they would be hung. This required the weaver to work at the loom with the image turned sideways, a technical feat in both planning and execution that establishes the Kalianda weavers as foremost in the ship cloth tradition.

While we can witness the decline and finally the end of the ship cloth tradition, we may never know how it evolved. Its predecessors are hard to find. Did it develop from some already established, sophisticated art forms? It is interesting that elements typical of Javanese culture appear in the ship cloths. Some would identify this as Javanese influence, others as an indication of a common cultural and historical pool shared by both Lampung and Java.[73] Ships were already important as images in Java in the ninth century, as the ship reliefs of Borobudur demonstrate. But any possible connections between these and the cloth tradition are obscure.

A further question concerns the relationship of these cloths to similar imagery or forms executed in other materials such as the ships on plaitwork mats from the same region (fig. 13, p. 13). Motifs burned on *lampit* (fig. 12, p. 11) are also similar to ship cloth motifs but not obviously structured in the same ways, although the mats are used in conjunction with *tampan* in many ceremonies. Most intriguing are the rare beaded *tampan maju* and beaded *palepai* (fig. 24, p. 18-19). They have some features in common with their woven counterparts but until more is learned, they will remain a mystery.

Fig. 47: A "red ship style" palepai *from Kalianda where the ships form a symmetrically balanced pair, although differing in small details, coloring, and form. Late 19th or early 20th century; warp 290 cm, weft 64 cm. Collection: Manring.*

Fig. 48: A "blue ship style" palepai *from the Semangka Bay area with a typical three-part subdivision of the ship's deck, each division including an architectural element. Late 19th or early 20th century; warp 250 cm, weft 63 cm; overall size: warp 250 cm, weft 128 cm. Collection: Manring.*

Fig. 49: Individual buildings in the five panels of this Kalianda palepai *may represent traditional clan houses,* lamban, *or village communal halls,* sesat, *that possibly once existed in the area. The skill required to weave five panels, with complex motifs oriented at right angles to the warp and hence to the view of the weaver, is remarkable. Late 19th or early 20th century; warp 380 cm, weft 79 cm. Collection: Manring.*

Fig. 50: The trees in this exceptionally complex five-paneled palepai *also resemble tiered ship forms or horns. Their hooked branches fill all available space around a central trunk decorated with medallions. While trees on ship cloths may generally represent a cosmic or world tree, some may also specifically represent the* kayu-ara, *a symbolic tree constructed of a pole, hung with mats, cloths, and gifts, and once made for marriage ceremonies in the Lampung region of Sumatra. Late 19th or early 20th century; warp 325 cm, weft 68 cm. Collection: Manring.*

Cloth Painting and Batik Traditions

There are a few textile traditions in Indonesia in which the color or dye for the pattern is directly painted or drawn on a foundation cloth. It may be a coincidence, but these traditions seem to occur among people such as the Toraja and Javanese who are also familiar with the batik technique and have historically placed a great importance on imported Indian textiles.

Batik was not made much outside Java, except in Jambi, East Sumatra, where it was probably introduced by Javanese immigrants.[74] In most areas there was little motivation to make batik because apparently it was easily available from Java through trade. Indeed, it was even made specifically for export to Sumatra and Bali.

There are puzzling, isolated instances of the use of the batik technique outside Java—in the Toraja country of southwestern Sulawesi. Here, rudimentary beeswax batik was made on long pieces of coarse cotton that were then incorporated into huge striped textiles, called *cawat cindako* or *topu baté* in the literature.[75] These were once associated with death rituals and headhunting (fig. 51). They are probably no longer made, but given their ceremonial use, they may have been a traditional textile of longstanding. More puzzling in both appearance and history are the *sarita*, long narrow ceremonial cloths in blue or brown on natural white. They appear to be similar in both proportion and design to the batik strip at the center of the *cawat cindako*. However, they seem to have been made in several techniques. From the 1880s, the Dutch manufactured (block printed?) blue and white *sarita* in Holland for export to Sulawesi where they found favor among some of the Eastern and Western Toraja, as head cloths and ceremonial dance garments. In southwestern Sulawesi *sarita* were apparently imitated by the Sa'dan Toraja, who stamped some with carved bamboo blocks, painted others freehand, and also used a batik technique (fig. 52, p. iii).[76] *Sarita* are made of finer cotton than the *cawat cindako*, but serve similar functions—as banners outside the houses of the deceased, as head cloths for the funeral effigies that rest in cliff burial chambers with the remains, and to encircle participants in sacred rites. It is not clear if there was ever an indigenous prototype for Dutch factory-made *sarita*, but whether their origin is foreign or indigenous, *sarita* are considered most holy.

Among the Sa'dan Toraja there is another category of holy textiles, known as *mawa* or *maa'*. The property of the nobility, this broad category includes imported Indian printed and painted cloths, European and other Indonesian textiles, and some cloths that were apparently painted locally. All came to be regarded as having a heavenly origin, given by the gods to protect man, his animals—especially the valued water buffalo—and his crops.[77] Locally-painted *mawa* exhibit many traditional themes from the Toraja environment similar to the schematic motifs on Toraja houses, but rendered far more freely (fig. 53).

*Fig. 51 (left): This extremely large, flag-like banner (*cawat cindako *or *topu baté*) was sometimes hung by the Toraja of Southwestern Sulawesi outside the house of an important deceased person during funerary rites. It is constructed unlike any other Indonesian textile. Thirty-three pieces of sturdy handspun, handwoven cotton are hemmed and joined in a patchwork, in which the central feature is a beeswax batik strip. The wax has been applied on one side in a rudimentary fashion, probably with a pointed section of split bamboo. Warp 400 cm, weft 136 cm. Collection: Manring.*

Fig. 53: Painted in soft tones of red-brown on white cotton, this mawa *represents one of the most sacred types of textiles of the Toraja. The crosses with filled centers apparently represent stars, a motif usually associated with a noblewoman. The keris in its sheath is also said to be a sign of a person of high standing. The buffalo surrounded by betel leaves is a frequently occuring theme, perhaps here representing an offering or gesture of hospitality. The two figures are possibly females who for certain Toraja ceremonies remain secluded in their houses, later being carried outside, entirely covered with their own* mawa. *Warp 288 cm, weft 73.5 cm. Collection: Summerfield.*

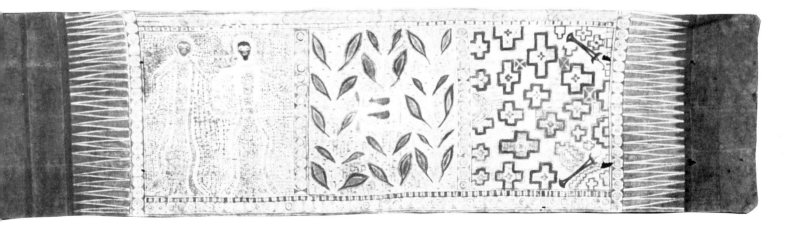

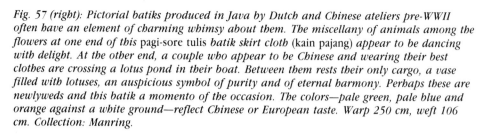

Differing in size, function, and design from Toraja batik, Javanese batik has a distinctive character that does not relate easily to the mainstream of Indonesian textiles. Indeed, the ritual textiles used in certain life-cycle ceremonies in both court and village communities in Java are not batiks but other cloths that may have deeper roots, for example, simple indigo and white plangi cloths, striped or plaid *lurik,* painted white cloth, and patchwork garments.[78] It is conceivable that these are fragments of a Javanese cloth tradition that predates batik as we know it. Seen in this way, the complex of batik patterns and garments, including court and dance costumes, is a relatively late development.

The evidence for early batik is inconclusive. The word was first recorded as "batick" in Dutch trade records in 1641.[79] It has not been found in any earlier Old Javanese sources. It is built on the root *tik,* referring to "drop," "dot," or "spot." It has been suggested, however, that it once applied to tattooing[80] and that it transferred to textiles patterned by a dotting technique. Indeed, there is one form of batik still practiced today that may reflect a long established form in which a pattern is composed entirely of individually applied dots.[81] In modern Javanese, the word *tulis* means writing and now refers to handwritten batiks on which the wax is applied with a *canting* tool. *Tulis,* by extension, refers to drawing and painting. The linear quality of some batiks and the dyeing of gradations of one color around the outline of a motif, as in Cirebon *megamendung* (cloud pattern) batiks, for example, suggest a direct link with painting and a similarity to Balinese traditional painting. This in turn probably derived to a large extent from Old Javanese painting. Together, these two concepts, derived from the ideas of "dot" and "writing," aptly describe the character of linear and dotted surface designs that are encompassed by the word batik today.

A thought-provoking Javanese perspective on the history of batik has recently been presented by batik scholar and designer, K. R. T. Hardjonagoro (1980). He argues that batik, in the costume forms that we know today, blossomed during the reign of Sultan Agung Hanyokrokusumo at Mataram in Central Java in the early seventeenth century. Further, he believes that batik is neither Islamic—because the religion has a proscription against the representation of living beings that conflicts with many batik motifs which include animals— nor Hindu-Buddhist—as that faith, having withdrawn into the courts, had ceased to influence or motivate the majority of Javanese. He suggests that when both these alien religions were on an uncertain footing, the one fading, the other just on the rise, the Javanese rediscovered their own traditional beliefs, the original philosophy of their ancestors, namely reverence for Batara Guru, the Creator, and unification of the male and female principles, *lingga* and *yoni.* Hardjonagoro believes that many Central Javanese batik motifs may be interpreted in the light of this philosophy as representing an offering to the Creator, and thus to fertility.

Hardjonagoro's theory might be applied to help explain the continuity of a core of well-established, well-recognized batik motifs from Central Java that we call "classic." The Central Javanese responded to the batik medium and adapted it to suit their philosophy and refined aesthetic. Making batik became a kind of semi-religious discipline. Generally, the classic motifs were best expressed in and preserved by the courts, that once sponsored the finest craftsmanship in all the traditional arts, reserving certain forms of batik for court use only. The conservative colors of blue, brown, black, and white (or cream) were used for motifs that range from geometrics and diagonals to the quintessentially Javanese *semen* patterns representing a cosmic landscape (fig. 54, p. iv). *Semen* has clear parallels with the sixteenth century East Javanese stone reliefs at Sendang Duwur, and similar forms also appear in the "garden" batiks of the court of Cirebon on the North Coast. In Central Java today, the processes of social change and economic development are such that fewer classic batiks of high quality are made or worn. In this respect, K. R. T. Hardjonagoro holds a special place, as one of the few creators of modern pieces that preserve the philosophy and spiritual feeling of the classic Javanese batik tradition (fig. 55).[82]

57

58

In other respects, Javanese batik is a hybrid. Motifs appear to have been inspired by every available source: simple plaitwork, weaving structures, and embroidery; historical Javanese architecture; traditional literature and painting; imported Indian *patola* silks; Chinese ceramics with phoenix birds, flowers, and auspicious symbols; European herbals and fairy tales. These motifs have been freely absorbed and elaborated. This freedom and flexibility has allowed batik to respond continually to new forms and colors (particularly colors introduced by chemical dyes) and to adapt to development by Dutch and Chinese outsiders, a characteristic that distinguishes it from the more conservative, restrained, and less changeable Javanese textiles.

On the North Coast, where batik became marvelously eclectic and varied, the processes of historical change have been felt strongly. Certain natural dye traditions disappeared with the widespread adoption of chemical dyes. Chinese-style batiks made on the North Coast developed several substyles, each with distinctive motifs and colors (fig. 56; fig. 57). After World War II, only a few of those substyles continued. The war also ended the domination by Dutch ateliers in the Pekalongan area that had developed in the first half of the century. Some areas such as Lasem, however, still continue their distinctive styles and colors, and there appears to be a healthy folk tradition of *tulis* batik (fig. 58) based on more conventional forms.

Fig. 56 (left): Among the Chinese communities on Java's North Coast many batik motifs and forms evolved to serve particular religious and ceremonial needs. This blue and white square is an uncommon size for batik, being too small for a traditional head cloth. It has been suggested that it is a cover for offerings or a cloth for a Chinese temple or household altar. Many Chinese motifs in the context of Indonesian art have multiple symbolic meanings, usually expressing good wishes of some kind—for longevity, health, happiness, prosperity, many and devoted male offspring, etc. The host of animals, objects, and illustrious personages emanating from the center of this textile may represent such auspicious signs. The spiral filled with figures may relate to spirals used by fortune tellers in China and to those found in woodblock folk prints used for children's dice games especially at the New Year. Pre-WWII; warp 58.5 cm, weft 64 cm. Collection: Summerfield.

Detail of Fig. 57, page 41.

Fig. 62: *Warp ikat is not the only patterning technique contained between warp stripes. The Sumbanese have mastered the time-consuming method of supplementary warp patterning for their noblewomen's ceremonial skirts (lau pahudu). The supplementary yarns are generally lighter in color and thicker than the plain-woven ground and appear in a contrasting twill-woven texture. These contrasts and the choice of strong figural imagery make the skirts outstanding examples of Indonesian textile art. The powerful figure, bare-headed, with a skeletal X-rayed rib cage, arms akimbo and knees barely flexed, represents a tau, a mature man. The "tree" with its tripartite leaf arrangement and its large edible tuber is an herb. The birds may be (wild?) chickens. Warp 126 cm, weft 146 cm. Collection: Moss.*

Traditional Techniques: Puzzles and Innovations

Important textiles are found in Indonesia, made with ingenuity and devoted craftsmanship and using techniques unusual enough to be singled out. Sometimes there occurs a small variation that gives a distinctive character to items from a particular area; at other times there is an outstanding technical innovation or development that raises more questions than it answers.

Like the Sumatrans in the Palembang-Jambi region and the Javanese, the Toraja in isolated, mountainous, southwestern Sulawesi are among the few groups in Indonesia to have employed all three basic resist techniques: ikat, batik, and plangi. Sometimes, by working on a large scale they have produced dramatic results: as well as long warp ikats and long batik banners, they have also made long plangi ceremonial textiles. In these, strong primary red and blue with white and a black over-dyed ground create bold elementary geometric forms, a total contrast to the fine silk plangi of Sumatra, Java, and Bali. In addition the Toraja also developed a resist dyeing technique with no obvious precursors, one that is not practiced elsewhere in Indonesia (fig. 59).[83] It involved the use of woven-slit openwork not only as a means of patterning but also as a way to guide the placement of resist bindings through the slits so that the piece could be tied and dyed after it was woven.

It appears that only the Balinese have produced or had an interest in using very loosely woven, light-weight textiles. Varying the density of the weave can have a marked effect on the finished textile. The *bebali* is a Balinese ceremonial cloth of polychrome weft ikat in which, instead of the firm weft-faced weave usually associated with weft ikat, the plain weave is very loose. In the body of the *bebali*, the single warps may number as few as fifteen to one inch, the single wefts twenty-four to one inch, with the result that the weft patterns become a soft elusive blur of color. The inspiration for the *bebali* may have been an attempt to imitate the soft loose weave of *patola*. The Balinese also used slit tapestry weave combined with spaced warps to achieve a particularly fragile lattice effect (fig. 60).

The Balinese inhabitants of the village of Tenganan Pageringsingan are the only people in the Archipelago to practice the demanding and time-consuming technique of double ikat, in their famous *geringsing*. Both warp yarns and weft yarns are measured out, bound with bast fiber resists to predetermined patterns, immersion dyed (sometimes over a period of years), unbound, and then woven with care so that the patterned warps are perfectly aligned and the patterned wefts perfectly integrated. Only thus will the patterns appear clearly. The finished pieces are sacred and have their prescribed ceremonial and ritual uses.[84] Certain *geringsing* motifs appear to be related to Javanese temple sculpture, although the relationship is as yet unexplained. *Geringsing* are also obviously influenced by *patola* both technically and in their use of certain floral-geometric motifs. However, many of their characteristics are probably Balinese developments: the use of cotton instead of silk; the distinctive colors (particularly the red-purple tone from red dyed over blue); the several cloth forms (all small); the practice of joining some of them into larger garments; and the prominent, plain white selvages with no patterned side borders or *tumpal* end borders.

Among the Bataks in North Sumatra, both weaving and dyeing traditions continue relatively strongly, a reflection of the deeply ingrained requirements for ritual cloth that continue to be part of the Batak way of life and death. Their best dyeing and weaving is subtle and dignified, particularly their warp ikats. Their use of the supplementary weft technique to make patterned white end panels in certain ceremonial shawls and shoulder cloths has unique aspects. The procedure sometimes involves changing the central warps from colored to white. With the help of a special frame, the colored and white warps are laid together, a few wefts are woven to secure the white, and then the colored warps are cut off. Tiny fringes mark

Fig. 60: In this Balinese weaving narrow white stripes between widely spaced warps make a subtle undercurrent to a stronger zig-zag pattern in soft tones of brown, yellow, light red, purple, and green. Each color change is clearly demarcated by the very wide slits in the tapestry weave, which, as negative space, add a repeating square element to the design. Loosely woven textiles similar to this were worn as breast cloths for attendance at temple festivals or making offerings at household shrines. Pre-WWII(?); warp 165 cm, weft 72 cm. Collection: Manring.

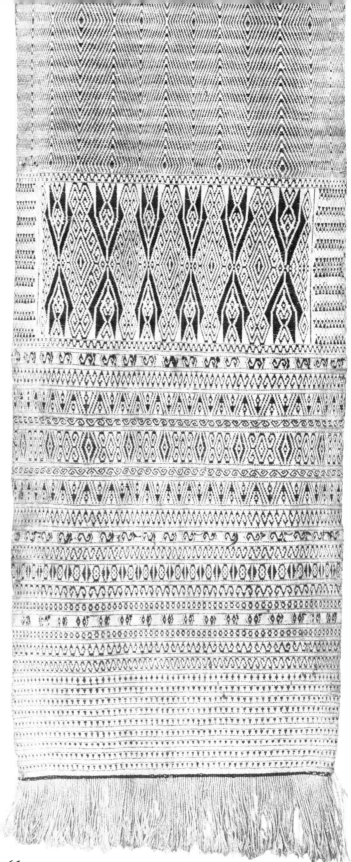

59

61

Fig. 59: *This uncommon type of head cloth from the Toraja in Sulawesi appears to be technically unique in Indonesia. A resist dyeing process is applied after weaving, using holes in the weave created by a woven-slit openwork technique to guide the placement of the resist bindings. The result is a double pattern effect: in silhouette the slits form a geometric pattern; in full light the agglomeration of the small rectangular white resisted areas creates a modest pattern of its own, visually subdividing the cloth into horizontal sections. This example is a soft, monochrome red. Late 19th or early 20th century; warp 292 cm, weft 27.3 cm. Collection: Summerfield.*

Fig. 61: *The entire surface of this head cloth or shoulder cloth from the Batak people of North Sumatra is densely patterned with detailed woven designs combining supplementary weft with a striped twill-woven centerfield—an excellent demonstration of the Batak woman's consummate weaving skills. Warp 235 cm, weft 29.5 cm. Collection: Manring.*

Fig. 64: The ceremonial costume of the Timor Atoni warrior once consisted of ikat skirt cloths, sashes, shoulder cloths, elaborate belts, a betel bag, a long sword, and large jewelry pieces. The narrow pilu saluf (left) would be wrapped round his head or waist. The larger fringed piece (right) could be tied at the waist or over the shoulder. In nineteenth century tribal society, when ritual headhunting was viewed as essential for bringing an influx of life energy to a community, this costume probably would have been considered magically powerful. Pre-WWII; apron: warp 70.5 cm, weft 34.5 cm; headband: warp 172 cm, weft 12.4 cm. Collection: Moss.

Fig. 63: The man's betel bag (aluk) has exceptional importance in Timor. This Tetum example is technically excellent, combining weft twining and supplementary weft wrapping with wrapped and beaded fringes. Pre-WWII; 70 x 21.5 cm without strap. Collection: Moss.

Fig. 65: This woman's cotton mourning hood (pote) is from the Sa'dan Toraja of Southwestern Sulawesi whose death ceremonies are associated with rituals of the west, the place where the sun dies. Black, the color of night, is also the color of mourning, thus the hood is somber and reserved. It is also a technical tour de force with woven-slit openwork, twining, braided fringes, and a tablet-woven band around its front edges. 125 x 44 cm. Collection: Manring.

this transition.[85] They also use a twill weave (fig. 61) and occasionally place narrow stripes with supplementary warp patterning in the side panels of certain cloths.

The supplementary warp technique is not common in Indonesia but occurs in widely separated areas, raising the question of how it might have been learned. Apart from the Batak example mentioned above and a few isolated examples in Bali, [86] Timor, [87] and East Flores, [88] it is not used as a principle means of patterning textiles except in Sumba where the ceremonial skirts of the noblewomen are sometimes patterned in this technique, occasionally combined with warp ikat and appliqué. To preserve the patterns, sets of pattern sticks are carefully preserved.[89] Among the most powerful motifs used are frontal anthropomorphic figures and several tree forms (fig. 62).

Supplementary weft wrapping done at the time of weaving is known particularly in Borneo and Timor. Among the Iban it is sometimes used as a main patterning technique on large pieces. Called sungkit, it is found on skirts, jackets, and sacred cloths called pua sungkit. It appears highly suited to the detailed nature of typical Iban surface design. In Timor, the same technique is used for a different effect, almost as a substitute for embroidery after weaving. It may be seen, for example, on small betel bags where, combined with other techniques such as twining and beadwork, it represents the epitome of excellent craftsmanship (fig. 63).

Certain textiles exhibit a combination of archaic techniques and unusual forms. Because weft elements are worked by hand into passive warps that do not even have to be mounted on a loom, weft twining is sometimes viewed as an archaic stage between plaitwork and weaving. It is widely used in the Archipelago, mainly for end bands that secure the fringes of textiles made by other techniques. A few garments, formerly associated with headhunting traditions, demonstrate more extensive use of the technique, among them, the pilu saluf from Timor, which combines slit tapestry weave and twining to form a strongly colored, tightly constructed, uniquely shaped piece (fig. 64).[90]

Tablet weaving is another archaic technique particularly suited to making narrow bands. It occurred in a few widely scattered locations—Sulawesi, Timor, and Java—and raises the unanswered question of how such a distribution arose. In Sulawesi the bands had numerous uses: as keris belts; as belts for the beaded apron, sassang (fig. 22, p. 16); as material for betel bags; as part of a Sa'dan Toraja woman's mourning hood. The cloth for the hood is woven and sewn with devoted skill, and a tablet-woven band is added around the entire edge as an extraordinary finishing touch (fig. 65).[91]

A Selection of Ceremonial Skirts

In almost every group in the Archipelago, the women make, or once made, ceremonial skirts according to their own traditional needs. Sometimes a woman's best dress consisted mainly of her skirt, complemented by her own or her clan's jewelry. Sometimes her skirt was the basic layer of an elaborate costume which might have included a blouse, fine shawl, or a shoulder cloth draped according to a traditional style. Skirts may not be the most ritually significant or magically powerful textiles, but the finest of them are eloquent and sometimes dynamic display pieces in their own right. They reveal a woman's wealth and status to both participants and observers in life-cycle ceremonies and provide a beautiful sight for the pleasure and enjoyment of the local deities or ancestors.

The wealth that came to the Lampung region of South Sumatra as a result of the pepper trade with the Dutch was partially spent on extravagant ceremonial costume and jewelry, particularly that worn by young unmarried women.[92] Beneath the glitter of applied mirror pieces, couched gold yarns, and shining embroidery silks, the long ceremonial tube skirts, *tapis,* embody materials, techniques, and motifs that have deep Indonesian roots. The foundation cloth was locally spun and woven cotton, or, occasionally, imported silk, or a silk and cotton combination. It was divided into broad warp stripes, some of which carried warp ikat, embroidery in colored silks, couched metallic yarns, appliqué, or supplementary weft patterning with metallic yarns. Two or more techniques would be combined within one *tapis,* the choice and the motifs varying according to local areas within the region. Warp ikat, in brown, yellow-orange, or red, was combined with silk embroidery in the inland and mountainous areas (fig. 66; fig. 67). Sometimes embroidered motifs were present without ikat but with appliqué. In the southern and southeastern coastal areas there was more emphasis on

Fig. 70 (left): The Tetum women of Timor excel at very fine, densely patterned, and highly detailed warp ikat. Here the center stripes of a ceremonial skirt carry concentric lozenge-and-hook motifs that act as a quiet foil to the end panels with their exuberant stepped lozenges worked in supplementary weft wrapping in silk. Pre-WWII; warp 124 cm, weft 164 cm. Collection: Moss.

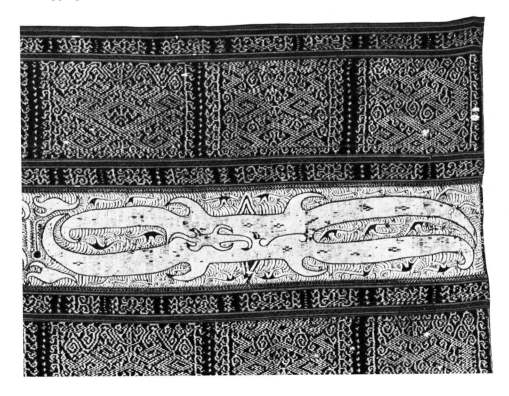

Fig. 66: A band of free-form, white satin stitch embroidery contrasts with the orderly brown warp ikat of this (opened) tube skirt, from inland South Sumatra. The large mysterious embroidered figures have been called cumi cumi, *squid or cuttlefish in Indonesian, but this may be a label of convenience without supporting field data. One explanation given for the contrasting styles is that the embroidery was designed by young men who had it carried out by the girls they were courting. Thus it reflected the sinuous and curvilinear characteristics of men's designs as seen elsewhere on wood carving, while the warp ikat reflected women's weaving traditions. Late 19th or early 20th century; warp 138 cm, weft 127 cm. Collection: Manring.*

Detail of Fig. 67 opposite.

Fig. 67: A wide embroidered band of this warp ikat Lampung tube skirt (tapis) is densely packed with elaborate ships. Important passengers are framed by trees and banners. The ship forms have so many compartments and projections that they begin to take on aspects of proliferating flora. Late 19th or early 20 century; warp 127 cm, weft 127 cm. Collection: Manring.

Fig. 68: The major embroidery band in this Lampung tapis has sets of paired white lotus (?) blossoms on long stalks. It is overshadowed by flanking bands of geometric forms in gold metallic yarns in supplementary weft—a reflection of a taste for elaborate display. Pre-WWII; warp 127 cm, weft 63 cm (half only). Collection: Manring.

display and hence a preference for gold metallic yarns, either couched or woven in (fig. 68). On the west coast, *tapis* were made carrying an extraordinary number of applied mirror pieces, and a small jacket was made to match. The basic colors of the *tapis*—indigo, several shades of red, red-brown, brown, and yellow sometimes derived from turmeric—are traditionally Indonesian, while the motifs collectively form a microcosm of major Indonesian textile designs. Framed in the warp ikat are suggestions of trees, human figures within schematic forms, and hook-and-key motifs similar to those found on Timor and Toraja textiles, all embedded in curling tendrils reminiscent of the densely packed design surfaces on Iban warp ikats. In the embroidered stripes are creatures of the sea, tendrils and blooming lotus meanders, and high prowed, multi-decked ships with passengers, banners, and flags. In addition to the ships, there are motifs that are unexplained and totally mysterious. Unfortunately, they must remain thus, as, except for some commercial pieces, these magnificent skirts have not been made for many years.

The island of Timor had at least one highly valued commodity, sandalwood, which brought it early into the sphere of international maritime commerce. Silk was probably among the trade goods exchanged, which might explain its presence today in Timor textiles that otherwise seem relatively unaffected by the outside world. Silk was used sparingly, as an occasional bright stripe or pattern detail worked in a supplementary technique. The Tetum women of Central Timor made one of the most successful uses of it in long cotton ceremonial tube skirts, which combined polychrome silk supplementary weft wrapping with the fine two-color warp ikat specific to the Tetum. This combination blends warp stripe traditions with silk traditions; the same dualism is found in the Lampung *tapis.*

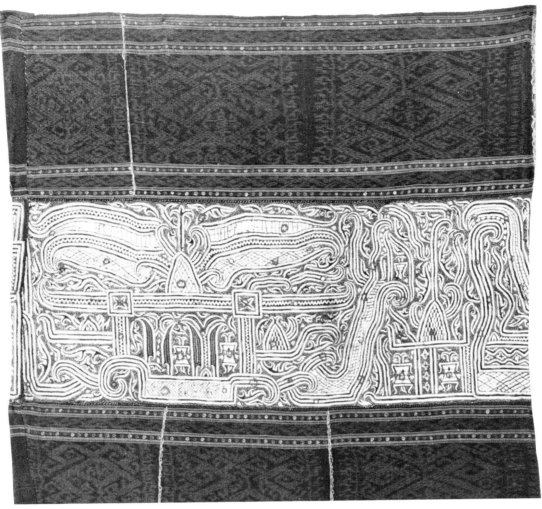

67

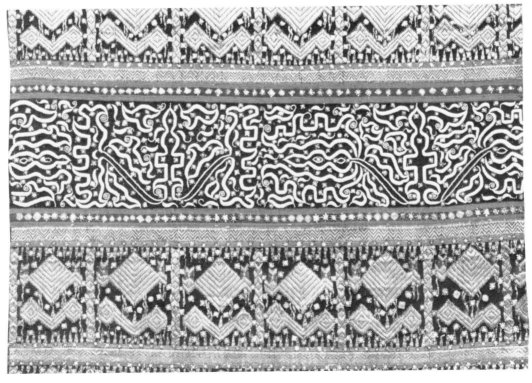

68

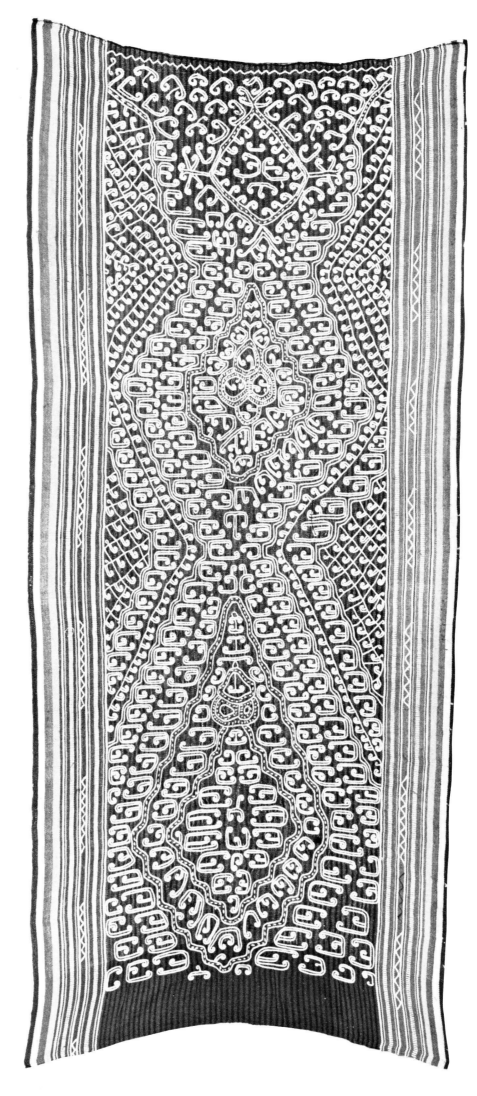

Although described relatively early by ethnographers recording ceremonial events, [93] Tetum skirts have since received relatively little attention in the textile literature. Their silk motifs exhibit considerable variety, from representations of lizards (fig. 69, cover) and crocodiles to anthropomorphic and geometric (fig. 70) figures. Within the restraints imposed by the wrapping technique, which requires the weaver to follow the general weft direction of the yarns as she works, thereby creating a stepped quality, the flexibility of the forms is considerable. When worn, for example, at the *likuri* dance, a round dance in which a line of festively clad women carry small drums to beat the rhythm, the skirt is drawn up under the arms, the excess being folded over and secured. With an elaborate headdress, it makes an impressive display.

When the Iban women put on their short ikat skirts, they do so only for special parts of a ceremony, for example, when they are making offerings to ancestral spirits or deities, who will be pleased by their display. According to one legend, certain spirit ancestors once came to visit an Iban woman. They saw her making an everyday black skirt and became angry, scolding her for not making an attractive pattern. A quarrel followed; the Iban were separated from their spirit ancestors, who thereafter visited them only in dreams; the woman who was scolded tried everafter to make beautifully patterned fabrics. [94] Tying and dyeing the designs for Iban ikats is a serious matter that is carried out under ritual conditions, especially if new designs are being created that have been received from ancestors in dreams. In general, ikat patterns are considered to have a beneficial or protective character. One and one-half pattern repeats are generally used for the skirts (fig. 71), although there does not appear to be a particular explanation for this unusual pattern division. Besides providing the wearer with the protection or powers believed to be embodied in the designs, Iban skirts also demonstrated the skills of the maker and, when worn with the weight of jewelry typical of an Iban ensemble, must surely have been part of a display of wealth. The application to the skirts of additional materials such as red cloth, gold paper, sequins, bells, coins, etc., would be a further source of pleasure for the deities. While warp ikat is the most commonly used patterning technique for Iban skirts, fine ceremonial skirts are also made in supplementary techniques like *pilih* and *sungkit,* and with embroidery (fig. 72). Care invested in their making suggests that, like the ikat skirts, these were also to please the gods.

This selection of Indonesian ceremonial skirts provides examples of the ways Indonesian textiles give a human body both form and identity. In their broadest sense, Indonesian fabrics can also structure and define the space around people and even protect them, at the same time reflecting their cultural and personal characteristics. Indeed, such fabrics provide a powerful language of color, texture, and image that clearly expresses the remarkable aesthetic of the Indonesian peoples.

NOTES

[1] Irene Emery, *The Primary Structures of Fabrics: An Illustrated Classification* (Washington: Textile Museum, 1966), xvi.

[2] Peter Gathercole, Adrienne L. Kaeppler, and Douglas Newton, *The Art of the Pacific Islands* (Washington: National Gallery of Art, 1979), 150.

[3] Wilhelm G. Solheim, II, Barbara Harrisson, and Lindsey Wall, "Niah 'Three Color Ware' and Related Prehistoric Pottery from Borneo," *Asian Perspectives* 3 (1959): 167-176 and pl. i-ix.

[4] James Willis in association with Mort Dimondstein, *Sculpture of the Batak, May 15-June 30, 1979* (San Francisco: James Willis Gallery, 1979), 24.

[5] John E. Vollmer, "Archaeological Evidence for Looms from Yunnan," in *Looms and Their Products: Irene Emery Roundtable on Museum Textiles, 1977 Proceedings,* ed., Irene Emery and Patricia Fiske (Washington: Textile Museum, 1979), 78-80.

[6] Marie Jeanne Adams, "A 'Forgotten' Bronze Ship and a Recently Discovered Bronze Weaver from Eastern Indonesia: A Problem Paper," *Asian Perspectives* 20 (1977): 92.

[7] Ibid.

[8] A. J. Bernet Kempers, *Ageless Borobudur* (Wassenaar: Servire, 1976), 241.

[9] Vollmer, "Archaeological Evidence for Looms," 80, 85.

[10] Joyce C. White, *Ban Chiang: Discovery of a Lost Bronze Age* (Philadelphia: University Museum, University of Pennsylvania, and the Smithsonian Institution Traveling Exhibition Service, 1982), 76.

[11] Rubellite K. Johnson and Bryce G. Decker, "Implications of the Distribution of Names for Cotton (*Gossypium* spp.) in the Indo-Pacific," *Asian Perspectives* 23 (1980): 296.

[12] Wolfgang Marschall, "On the Stone Age of Indonesia," *Tribus* 23 (1974): 85-87.

[13] Wilhelm G. Solheim, II, "Philippine Prehistory," in *People and Art of the Philippines* (Los Angeles: Museum of Cultural History, University of California, 1981), 44, 46.

[14] Theodore G. Th. Pigeaud, *Java in the Fourteenth Century: A Study in Cultural History* 5 vols. (The Hague: Martinus Nijhoff, 1960-1963), 3:148; 4:390.

[15] W. P. Groeneveldt, *Historical Notes on Indonesia and Malaya Compiled from Chinese Sources* (1880; reprint, Djakarta: C. V. Bharatara, 1960), 55.

[16] Theodore G. Th. Pigeaud, *Literature of Java* (The Hague: Martinus Nijhoff, 1967), 1:35.

[17] Brian E. Colless, "Majapahit Revisited: External Evidence on the Geography and Ethnology of East Java in the Majapahit Period," *Journal of the Malay Branch of the Royal Asiatic Society* 48 (1975): 124-161.

[18] Anthony Forge, *Balinese Traditional Paintings: A Selection from the Forge Collection of the Australian Museum, Sydney* (Sydney: Australian Museum, 1978), 9.

[19] S. Kooijman, *Ornamented Bark-Cloth in Indonesia,* Mededelingen van het Rijksmuseum voor Volkenkunde, Leiden, no. 16 (Leiden: E. J. Brill, 1963), 63-65.

[20] Robin Hanbury-Tension, *A Pattern of Peoples: Journey Among the Tribes of Indonesia's Outer Islands* (New York: Charles Scribner's Sons, 1975), pl. between 96-97.

[21] Wanda Warming and Michael Gaworski, *The World of Indonesian Textiles* (Tokyo: Kodansha, 1981), 55-56.

[22] Hans Schärer, *Ngaju Religion: The Conception of God Among a South Borneo People,* Koninklijk Instituut voor Taal-, Land- en Volkenkunde Translation Series, no. 6 (The Hague: Martinus Nijhoff, 1963), 89-90.

[23] N. Adriani and Albert C. Kruyt, *De Bare'e sprekende Toradjas van Midden-Celebes (de Oost-Toradjas)/The Bare'e-Speaking Toradja of Central Celebes (the East Toradja),* trans. of 1951 2nd ed. Jenni Karding Moulton (New Haven: Human Relations Area Files, 1970-1971), 3:454.

[24] Ibid., 414

[25] Kooijman, *Ornamented Bark-Cloth in Indonesia,* 18-19.

[26] Walter Kaudern, *Art in Central Celebes,* vol. 6 of *Ethnographical Studies in Celebes* (Göteborg: Etnografska Museet, 1944), 173-175.

[27] Tom Harrisson, "Early dates for 'Seated' Burial and Burial Matting at Niah Caves, Sarawak (Borneo)," *Asian Perspectives* 18 (1975): 162.

[28] Groeneveldt, *Historical Notes on Indonesia and Malaya,* 13.

[29] Ibid., 17

[30] Brian E. Colless, *"Majapahit Revisited,"* 154.

[31] Schärer, *Ngaju Religion,* 12-17.

[32]Indonesisch Ethnografisch Museum, Delft, *Kalimantan mythe en kunst: tentoonstelling Februari 1973-December 1973* (Delft: Indonesisch Ethnografisch Museum, 1973), 168-170, 173.

[33]Schärer, *Ngaju Religion,* 83.

[34]Harley Harris Bartlett, *The Labors of the Datoe: And Other Essays on the Bataks of Asahan (North Sumatra),* Michigan papers on South and Southeast Asia, no. 5 (Ann Arbor: Center for South and Southeast Asian Studies, University of Michigan, 1973), 152-153.

[35]Ibid., 192-193, 182-183.

[36]Lucas Chin, *Cultural Heritage of Sarawak* (Kuching: Sarawak Museum, 1980), 70, 73.

[37]Mattiebelle Gittinger, "A Study of the Ship Cloths of South Sumatra: Their Design and Usage" (Ph.D. Diss., Columbia University, New York, 1972; reprint, Ann Arbor: Xerox University Microfilms, 1975), 56-60, 62-64, 66-68.

[38]J. E. Jasper and Mas Pirngadie, *Het Vechtwerk,* Vol. 13 of *De Inlandsche Kunstijverheid in Nederlandsch Indië* (The Hague: Mouton, 1912), 219-220. C. H. M. Palm, "De Cultuur en Kunst van de Lampung, Sumatra," *Kulturpatronen,* 7 (1965): 40-79.

[39]J. Dumarçay, "Les Charpentes Figurées de Prambanan," *Archipel* 7 (1974): pl. opp. 129.

[40]Suellen Glashausser and Carol Westfall, *Plaiting Step-By-Step* (New York: Watson-Guptill, 1976), 22.

[41]Georg Buschan, *Die Sitten der Völker* (Stuttgart: Union Deutsche Verlagsgesellschaft, n.d.), 1:11.

[42]H. H. Juynboll, *Molukken II,* vol. 22 of *Catalogus van Rijks Ethnographisch Museum* (Leiden: E. J. Brill, 1931), 100-101.

[43]Urs Ramseyer, *The Art and Culture of Bali* (Oxford: Oxford University Press, 1977), 164, fig. 208.

[44]Ibid., 153.

[45]Ibid., fig. 216.

[46]Laurens Langewis, "Lamak: A Woven Balinese Lamak," in *Lamak and Malat in Bali and a Sumba Loom* (Amsterdam: Royal Tropical Institute, 1956), 31-47, figs. 6-16.

[47]Solheim, II, "Philippine Prehistory," 32.

[48]Adelheid Munan-Oettli, "Bead Cap 64/88 in the Sarawak Museum Collection," *Sarawak Museum Journal* 32 (n.s. 53) (1983): 89-96, pl xvi-xviii.

[49]Walter Kaudern, *Art in Central Celebes, Ethnographical Studies in Celebes,* Volume 16 (Göteborg: Ethnografska Museet, 1944), 271-272.

[50]Hedda Morrison, *Life in a Longhouse* (N.p.: Borneo Literature Bureau, 1962), 178.

[51]Mattiebelle Gittinger, *Splendid Symbols: Textiles and Tradition in Indonesia* (Washington: Textile Museum, 1979), 74, 97.

[52]Nigel Bullough, *Woven Treasures from Insular Southeast Asia* (Auckland: Auckland Institute and Museum, 1981), pl. vii.

[53]Gittinger, *Splendid Symbols,* 97.

[54]John Maxwell, "Textiles of the Kapuas Basin—With Special Reference to Maloh Beadwork," in *Indonesian Textiles:* Irene Emery Roundtable, 1979 Proceedings. ed. Mattiebelle Gittinger (Washington: Textile Museum, 1980), 127-140.

[55]Rita Bolland and A. Polak, "Manufacture and Use of Some Sacred Woven Fabrics in a North-Lombok Community," *Tropical Man* 4 (1971): 149-170.

[56]E. P. Patanne, "Rediscovery of Southeast Asia," *Orientations* 3 (1972): 42; and Solheim, "Philippine Prehistory," 78-79.

[57]Robyn J. Maxwell, "Textiles and Tusks: Some Observations on the Social Dimensions of Weaving in East Flores," in *Five Essays on the Indonesian Arts* (N. P.: Monash University, 1981), 48.

[58]Alfred Bühler, "Patola Influences in Southeast Asia," *Journal of Indian Textile History,* 4 (1959): 4-46.

[59]James J. Fox, "Roti, Ndao, Savu," in *Textile Traditions of Indonesia,* ed. Mary Hunt Kahlenberg (Los Angeles: Los Angeles County Museum of Art, 1977), 98.

[60]Anita Spertus and Jeff Holmgren, "Celebes," in *Textile Traditions of Indonesia,* ed. Kahlenberg, 53.

[61]Ibid., 54.

[62]Marie Jeanne Adams, *System and Meaning in East Sumba Textile Design: A Study in Traditional Indonesian Art,* Cultural Report Series, no. 16 (New Haven: Yale University, Southeast Asia Studies, 1969).

[63]Groeneveldt, *Historical Notes on Indonesia and Malaya,* 80.

[64]O. W. Wolters, *Early Indonesian Commerce: A Study of the Origins of Śrīvijaya* (Ithaca: Cornell University Press, 1967), 201.

[65]Ibid., 78-79.

[66]Ibid., 153.

[67]Groeneveldt, *Historical Notes on Indonesia and Malaya,* 16.

[68]J. C. van Leur, *Indonesian Trade and Society: Essays in Asian Social and Economic History* (The Hague: W. van Hoeve, 1967), 3.

[69]Kristof Glamann, *Dutch-Asiatic Trade 1620-1740* (The Hague: Martinus Nijhoff, 1981), 112-131.

[70]Gittinger, *Splendid Symbols,* 113.

[71]Gittinger, "A Study of the Ship Cloths of South Sumatra."

[72]Robert J. Holmgren and Anita E. Spertus, "Tampan Pasisir: Pictorial Documents of an Ancient Indonesian Coastal Culture," in *Indonesian Textiles,* ed. Gittinger, 157-198.

[73]Ibid., 176-180.

[74]Gittinger, *Splendid Symbols,* 110.

[75]Marie-Louise Nabholz-Kartaschoff, *Batik: Formen und Verbreitung eines Reserverfahrens zur Musterung von Textilien* (Basel: Museum für Völkerkunde und Schweizerische Museum für Volkskunde, 1970), 9-10, 32; J. W. van Nouhuys, "Was-batik in Midden Celebes," *Nederlandsch-Indië Oud en Niew,* 10 (1925-26): 110-122.

[76]Hetty Nooy-Palm, "The Role of the Sacred Cloths in the Mythology and Ritual of the Sa'dan-Toraja of Sulawesi, Indonesia," in *Indonesian Textiles,* ed. Gittinger, 81, 83.

[77]Ibid., 85.

[78]K. R. T. Hardjonagoro, "The Place of Batik in the History and Philosophy of Javanese Textiles," trans. R. J. Holmgren, in *Indonesian Textiles,* ed. Gittinger, 227-228.

[79]Gittinger, *Splendid Symbols,* 16.

[80]J. W. van Nouhuys, "Was-batik in Midden-Celebes," 121.

[81]Bronwen and Garrett Solyom, "Notes and Observations on Indonesian Textiles," in *Threads of Tradition: Textiles of Indonesia and Sarawak,* ed. Joseph Fischer (Berkeley: Lowie Museum of Anthropology, University of California, 1979): 22, 25.

[82]Hardjonagoro, "The Place of Batik," 235.

[83]J. H. Jager Gerlings, *Sprekende Weefsels: Studie over Onstaan en Betekenis van Weefsels van Enige Indonesische Eilanden* (Amsterdam: Koninklijk Instituut voor de Tropen, 1952), 40-42, Afb 13 &14. Nouhuys "Was-Batik in Midden-Celebes," 116.

[84]Alfred Bühler, Urs Ramseyer, and Nicole Ramseyer-Gygi, *Patola und Geringsing: Zeremonialtücher aus Indien und Indonesien* (Basel: Museum für Völkerkunde und Schweizerische Museum für Volkskunde, 1975).

[85]Mattiebelle Gittinger, "Selected Batak Textiles: Technique and Function," *Textile Museum Journal* 4 (1975): 14-15.

[86]Langewis, "Lamak."

[87]Gittinger, *Splendid Symbols,* 182-183.

[88]Robyn J. Maxwell, "Textiles and Tusks: Some Observations on the Social Dimensions of Weaving in East Flores," in *Five Essays on the Indonesian Arts* (N.p. Monash University. 1981), 45, 47.

[89]Adams, *System and Meaning,* 82-84; Rita Bolland, "Weaving a Sumba Woman's Skirt," in *Lamak and Malat in Bali and a Sumba Loom* (Amsterdam: Royal Tropical Institute, 1956), 49-56, figs. 17-21.

[90]C. Nooteboom, "Quelques Techniques de Tissage des Petites Îles de la Sonde," *Mededelingen van het Rijksmuseum voor Volkenkunde, Leiden,* 3 (1948), 1-100.

[91]Rita Bolland, "Three Looms for Tablet Weaving," *Tropical Man* 3 (1970): 176-178.

[92]C. H. M. Palm, "De Cultuur en Kunst van de Lampung, Sumatra:" 44-46, 73.

[93]B. A. G. Vroklage, *Ethnographie der Belu in Zentral-Timor,* vol. 3 (Leiden: E. J. Brill, 1953), pl. 76-77, pl. 80-81.

[94]Cornelia Volgelsanger, "A Sight for the Gods: Notes on the Social and Religious Meaning of Iban Ritual Fabrics," in *Indonesian Textiles,* ed. Gittinger, 118-119.

GLOSSARY

abaca. Philippine name for fiber from leaf sheath of species of banana, *Musa textilis.* Also known as Manilla hemp or *kofo.*

adat. Body of beliefs and customs traditionally regulating social and religious behavior of individuals and communities.

appliqué. Superimposition of small areas of accessory fabric on a ground fabric, with either stitchery or adhesive, for patterning rather than patching purposes (Emery 1966, 251).

badan. "Body" area(s) of a sarong adjacent to and usually patterned less elaborately than the *kepala.*

bark-cloth. Fabric made from inner bark, i.e., bast, of suitable trees or shrubs, softened, flattened, felted, and smoothed by soaking and beating (Emery 1966, 20).

bast fiber. Fiber obtained from stem structures of dicotyledonous plants, e.g., flax, jute, hemp, etc. (Emery 1966, 5).

batik. Resist dyeing process. Hot wax or rice paste resist is applied to fabric surface with various tools. Resist is boiled or scraped away after dyeing. For each color, partial or complete removal and reapplication of resist is required. See *cap* and *canting.*

bobbin lace. Lace made with several individual threads wound on bobbins to facilitate their manipulation into twined or interlaced structures (Emery 1966, 56, 67).

body-tension loom. Also called back-strap loom. Two-bar, frameless loom. Belt passing around weaver's back, secured to breast beam, is used to control tension of yarns as weaver leans forward or back. Warp beam is usually secured to house post, tree, etc.; less commonly it is braced against weaver's feet.

canting. Tool for applying wax to cloth for making batik *tulis.* Copper reservoir with spout(s), secured to small handle.

cap. Stamp, usually constructed of strips of sheet copper, used to apply wax for making batik.

cawat cindako. Large cloth with batik-patterned center stripe, used by the Toraja of southwestern Sulawesi.

ceplokan. Group of geometric Javanese batik patterns consisting of grids of circles, lozenges, squares, etc.

cili. Female figure with hourglass form and fan-shaped headdress, found on many Balinese works of art, and representing Dewi Sri, goddess of rice and fertility.

continuous supplementary weft. Supplementary weft patterning in which extra weft yarns are carried back and forth across the full width of the fabric (Emery 1966, 141).

couching. Threads are laid on fabric surface and stitched down with short stitches, which themselves may be arranged or colored to create a pattern.

daluwang. Old Javanese word for bark-cloth, bark-cloth clothing, or bark-cloth head cloth.

discontinuous supplementary weft. Supplementary weft patterning in which extra weft yarns are worked back and forth across limited areas of warp to shape pattern units (Emery 1966, 141).

double ikat. Ikat process applied to both warp and weft yarns. See ikat.

fabric. Generic term for all fibrous constructions, from Latin *fabricare,* to make, build, or fabricate. Distinguished from textile (Emery 1966, xvi).

float. Warp or weft element traveling over or under two or more of the opposite elements.

fuya. Bark-cloth, perhaps a corruption of *wuyang,* referring to bark-cloth skirt once made by the Minahassa of northern Sulawesi.

geringsing. Sacred double ikat textiles made only in the village of Tenganan Pageringsingan, east Bali.

gunungan. Mountain-tree form, symbolizing the cosmic realm where *wayang* dramas are set, represented in puppet form, sculpture, and on textiles.

hinggi. Sumbanese man's warp ikat shoulder or waist cloth. *Hinggi kawuru,* cloth dyed with indigo only. *Hinggi kombu,* cloth also dyed with red-brown made from *Morinda citrifolia.*

ikat. Resist dyeing process. Warp or weft yarns (or both) are measured out, bound to a preconceived pattern with dye-resistant material, and dyed. For each color, additional tying or partial removal of bindings is required. After last dyeing, all bindings are removed and yarns are ready for weaving.

interlocking tapestry weave. Tapestry weave in which the discontinuous wefts forming each adjacent area of color are turned around each other, leaving no slits in the weave. (Emery 1966, 80-81).

kain. "Cloth" in general, specifically various rectangular textiles with their own names, e.g. *kain panjang.*

kain panjang. "Long cloth," rectangular batik worn wrapped as ankle-length skirt.

kepala. "Head," focal section of a sarong with contrasting or more elaborate pattern than rest of cloth. See *badan.*

keris. Traditional Indonesian heirloom dagger, believed to have its own spirit and considered an essential possession of a mature man; may also symbolize a ruler's power and prestige.

kofo. See *abaca.*

lamak. Long rectangular hanging, made of cut and pinned palm leaves, rarely of woven cloth, for Balinese altars, shrines, temple gates, etc.

lampit. Mat of split *rotan,* known from Lampung region, Sarawak, and Java. Some Sumatran *lampit* have pyrographic designs.

lurik. Traditional multi-purpose Javanese cotton textiles patterned in stripes and plaids.

mawa. Sacred heirloom textiles, imported or locally made in a variety of techniques, used on ritual occasions by the Sa'dan Toraja of southwestern Sulawesi.

metallic yarns. Some consist of thin sheets of gold, silver, or copper alloy cut into narrow strips and wound round a core thread of silk, cotton, or bast. In others, thin metal sheet was applied to paper (sometimes treated with fine red clay to provide a smooth surface for the metal) before being cut into strips and wound round the core.

Morinda citrifolia. Tree, called *mengkudu* in Indonesian, from whose roots red dye, *kombu* or *kumbu,* is obtained.

naga. Serpent, snake or dragon believed to have magic powers; also a symbol of water and the lower world.

pagi-sore. "Morning-afternoon," refers to batik *kain panjang* with contrasting patterns in each half.

palepai. Long, rectangular, ceremonial ship cloth, used by aristocracy in South Lampung region.

patola. Silk double ikat textiles made in Gujarat, India, and exported throughout Southeast Asia for centuries. The most highly valued and influential of all trade cloths.

pilih. Term used in Borneo for a continuous supplementary weft technique in which long supplementary weft floats form the background, while the pattern is executed in the ground weave that anchors the floats.

plain weave. Basic weaving structure where warp and weft interlace over-one-under-one.

plangi. Resist dyeing process. Areas of cloth are knotted or tied with dye-resistant material, then dyed. For each color, additional tying or partial removal of resists is required. Resulting patterns are usually built of concentric circles or squares.

pua. Cloths, usually warp ikat, made by the Iban of Sarawak, used as hangings or shawls for ceremonial or ritual occasions. Sometimes called *pua kumbu* for the red dye used, from *Morinda citrifolia.*

resist dyeing. Any dyeing processes that employ dye-resistant materials to block penetration of dye on selected areas of a fabric surface, or on yarns prior to weaving. See batik, ikat, plangi, tritik.

rotan. Rattan, fiber from the stems of various climbing palms of the genus *Calamus* used for mats, basketry, etc.

sarong. Rectangular cloth sewn into a tube, worn various ways by men and women throughout Indonesia. Patterning may be divided into *kepala* and *badan.*

sassang. Ceremonial apron with open network of beading suspended from narrow waistband.

ship cloth. Name of convenience for ceremonial textiles once woven, in supplementary weft technique, in South Sumatra. Ships were only one of many motifs. See *tampan, tatibin, palepai.*

slit tapestry weave. Tapestry weave in which adjacent areas of color are separated by slits, the discontinuous wefts being turned around adjacent warps (Emery 1966, 79).

soga. Brown dye used in Javanese batik, derived from a combination of bark and wood from several trees.

sungkit. Term used in Borneo for supplementary weft wrapping technique in which discontinuous supplementary wefts are wrapped progressively around and across the warps, possibly with a needle.

supplementary weft. Form of extra-weft patterning in which weft yarns are woven into a textile to create patterns additional to the ground weave (Emery 1966, 140-143).

tablet weaving. Warps are threaded through hole-punched cards or tablets that are turned to create openings for weft to pass through. Suited for making narrow bands.

tampan. Small rectangular or square ship cloth from South Sumatra.

tapestry weave. Weft-faced plain weave, with discontinuous wefts, usually of different colors, woven back and forth within their own pattern areas (Emery 1966, 78).

tapis. General term for skirt cloth or sarong, including heavy ceremonial skirts of women from Lampung region.

tatibin. Small version of long rectangular ship cloth of South Lampung region.

textile. Specific term for woven (i.e. interlaced warp-weft) fabrics, from Latin *texere* to weave (Emery 1966, xvi).

tritik. Resist dyeing process. Cloth is stitched, gathered or tucked tightly so that dye cannot penetrate fully areas so drawn together. For each color, additional stitching or partial removal is required.

tulis. Indonesian and Javanese root for words related to writing, drawing and painting. Also batik in which pattern is hand-waxed, i.e. hand-drawn, with *canting.*

tumpal. Motif formed by row of repeating triangles, found in many Southeast Asian art forms, particularly as a border. Of ancient origin. Possibly represents a bud or mountain form.

twill weaves. Float weaves characterized by diagonal alignment of floats (Emery 1966, 92).

warp. Parallel elements that run longitudinally in a loom or fabric (Emery 1966, 74).

warp ikat. Ikat process applied only to warp yarns. See ikat.

wayang. Generic term for Javanese and Balinese theater forms, based mainly on Indonesianized versions of Hindu epics, told with puppets, with actors, and in art.

weft. Transverse elements of a fabric that cross and interwork with warp elements (Emery 1966, 74).

weft ikat. Ikat process applied only to weft yarns. See ikat.

weft twining. Two or more weft elements are spiraled around each other while encircling successive warps (Emery 1966, 200-203).

weft wrapping. Encircling or wrapping of warp elements by weft elements which are either the sole wefts in the fabric structure or supplementary to the ground weave (Emery 1966, 215).

woven-slit openwork. Patterning using discontinuous wefts to form systematic openings in the weave, when neither weft-faced weave nor different colored wefts occur (Emery 1966, 85).

Lenders to Exhibition

Don R. Bierlich, Los Angeles

Folk Art Gallery La Tienda, Seattle

Leslie Grace, Seattle

Henry Art Gallery Textiles Collection, University of Washington, Seattle
Collection of Ann Meerkerk (79.8-66, 79.8-68); Ann Meerkerk Estate (80.18-21);
loan of Sarah P. Bill (80.1000-3).

Mary Hunt Kahlenberg, Los Angeles

Mary Jane Leland, Los Angeles

Timothy and Tuti Manring, Seattle and Jakarta

Laurence A. G. Moss, Point Roberts, Washington

Museum of Cultural History, University of California at Los Angeles

Neutrogena Corporation, Los Angeles

Donald H. Rubinstein, Honolulu

Seattle Art Museum
Eugene Fuller Memorial Collection (40.80)

John and Anne Summerfield, Pacific Palisades

Menno van Wyk and V'Ella Warren, Federal Way, Washington

Private collection

Photography Credits

Marie Jeanne Adams, Cambridge, Massachusetts: 1
Robert J. Holmgren, New York: 13
Emmo Italiander, Jakarta: 23, 24, 27, 40, 46, 47, 50
Laurence A. G. Moss, Point Roberts, Washington: 15, 33, 39
Wilhelm G. Solheim II, Honolulu: 10
Garrett Solyom, Honolulu: 12, 14, 17, 20, 22, 28-32, 34, 35, 42, 51-55, 57, 59-61, 65-68, 72
Richard Todd, Los Angeles: 4, 11, 19, 21, 44, 45, 71
Thomas P. Vinetz, Los Angeles: 5, 8
Robert Vinnedge, Seattle: 3, 6, 7, 9, 18, 25, 26, 36, 37, 41, 43, 48, 49, 56, 58, 62, 63, 64, 69, 70
Menno van Wyk, Federal Way, Washington: 2, 16, 38

Exhibition Preparation

Patricia Grieve Watkinson, Curator and Acting Director
Bronwen and Garrett Solyom, Guest Curators
Museum staff: Margaret Johnson, Joyce Irwin, Michael Sletten, Suzanne LeBlanc

Publication Preparation

Designer: Jo Savage, Washington State University Press
Editors: Fred Bohm and Patricia Grieve Watkinson
Essay, glossary and cataloguing: Bronwen and Garrett Solyom
Printed by: Office of University Publications and Printing, Washington State University